P9-DWH-849

The Wines of Greece

FABER BOOKS ON WINE
General Editor: Julian Jeffs

Bordeaux (new edition) by David Peppercorn
Burgundy by Anthony Hanson
French Country Wines by Rosemary George
Port by George Robertson
Sherry by Julian Jeffs
Spirits and Liqueurs by Peter Hallgarten
The Wines of Portugal (new edition) by Jan Read
The Wines of the Rhône by John Livingstone-Learmonth and Melvyn C. H. Master
The Wines of Spain (new edition) by Jan Read
The Wines of Australia by Oliver Mayo
Drilling for Wine by Robin Yapp

THE WINES
OF
GREECE

MILES LAMBERT-GÓCS

faber and faber
LONDON · BOSTON

First published in 1990
by Faber and Faber Limited
3 Queen Square London WC1N 3AU

Phototypeset by Input Typesetting Ltd, London
Printed in Great Britain by
Clays Ltd, St Ives plc

British Library Cataloguing in Publication Data is available

ISBN 0–571–15387–9
ISBN 0–571–15388–7 (pbk)

For my friend,
Elias ('Louie') Sotirhos
of Seattle, Washington

It is thanks to Louie that I know that even in their most ordinary condition the modern Greeks have kept alive that special spark of the ancients. I learned it one day as we walked in a heavily forested and nearly deserted park half a world away from his native village below Parnassos. When I commented to Louie on the beauty of the place, he responded without a moment's hesitation, 'But no people today. The people is the beautiful.'

Ποτές μήν πιάνεσαι ἀπ'τά κλωνιά,
Πιάσου ἀπ'τόν κορμό

Never hold on by the shoots;
take hold of the stock.

proverb heard at Arakhova,
Central Greece

Contents

CONTENTS

Appendices

Illustrations

1 Samos (Eastern Sporades). Terraced vineyards of *moskháto áspro* in the north-central semi-mountainous zone.
2 Samos. A rainbow of muscat wine – from young dry wine from fresh grapes on the left, to aged sweet wine from partially raisined grapes on the right: Samian rosē is second from left.
3 Rhodes (Dodecanese). Plantings of *athíri* on the flanks of Mt Ataviros by Embonas.
4 Santorini (Cyclades). Vineyards on the island's inclined plateau, looking north from Fira.
5 Naousa (Macedonia). Rows of *xynómavro* at Yiannakokhori.
6 Rapsani (Thessaly). Vintage-time on the spines of Mt Kissavos, the Ossa of the ancients.
7 Nemea (Peloponnesos). *Ayioryítiko* ripening in 'the deep valley of Nemea' (Pindar, *The Nemean Odes*)
8 Cephalonia (Ionian Islands). View southwest towards the island capital of Argostoli, from *robóla* vineyards in the appellation zone near Dilinata.

Maps

═══

Author's Preface

———

I hope this book will be a useful guide and valued companion to Greek wine. The wines of Greece are as multifarious and fascinating as its geography, and well worth knowing and watching, especially now that more and more unique vintages are becoming available in bottle. Other wine countries have banked on an interested, informed, and appreciative foreign audience in updating their production of wine, and wine lovers the world over should want to help urge Greek producers to do their very best, to coax more wine-growers into bottling, and to bring about an upturn for wine at places not presently heard from because of unfortunate circumstances in recent times.

I have aimed to present the regional and local traditions in Greek wine so that wine lovers abroad can know what to expect and ask of places and producers. Furthermore, because individual producers and labels may come and go over the decades, it is particularly worth understanding the traditions they represent since those are a continuum by which faithful replacements can be recognized and encouraged.

While contemporary Greek wine is my focus, it has been hardly possible to avoid altogether Greece's ancient past in wine. For one thing, certain things seen and heard in Greek vineyards and cellars today are distinctly reminiscent of passages found in ancient literature and make them germane to an acquaintance with the background of contemporary wine. I have devoted a section to 'Classical Reflections' in each of the eleven regional chapters, as well as a chapter to what I think is a vital and relevant picture of Greek wine in antiquity. Since this chapter is an overview and the Classical Reflections sections are discussions of narrower topics suggested to me by the respective regions or their wines, readers with a special interest in wine history might find it particularly rewarding to read the chapter on wine and the Greeks during antiquity first and then to re-read it at the finish, even at the risk of allowing the larger-than-life ancients to commandeer the story of Greek wine, as can happen all too easily. I might draw special attention, too, to the Lexicon, largely intended as an exploration of the sensory language of the ancient Greeks, and which I believe has the merit of providing new perspectives on ancient wine, and also on our own language of wine appreciation.

Miles Lambert-Gócs
Alexandria, Virginia
October 1989

Acknowledgements

It would not have been possible to assemble the information I wanted about Greek wines without the cooperation of those who make them, and so I am very much indebted to all the producers who took the time to discuss their wine-making with me. However, I must single out Count Nikolaos Comoutos of Zakynthos for his extra effort in aiding my research.

Other persons in the Greek wine industry to whom I wish to express my appreciation are Dr Ulysses Davides, Professor Emeritus of the Department of Ampelology at the Superior College of Agriculture of Athens; Dr Stavroula Kourakou-Dragona, former Director of the Greek Wine Institute; Yiannis Boutaris, President of the Association of Greek Wine and Beverage Industries (SEVOP); and Dimitrios Kavour, General Director of the Central Union of Wine-producing Cooperative Organizations of Greece (KEOSOE).

Among the numerous individuals in various walks of life who facilitated my acquaintance with Greek wine regions, I would like to make special mention of Evangelos Katevenis of Samos; Pantelis Kefalas of Khios; Panayiotis Koritos of Arakhova, Central Greece; Yeoryios Itzkaras of Naousa, Macedonia; and John Ternas of Queens, New York.

For their help in arranging a variety of matters in support of this book, I also owe thanks to Nikolaos Efstathiadis, former Agricultural Counsellor of the Embassy of Greece in Washington, DC; Charalambos Machairidis, Greek Commercial Counsellor, Washington, DC, and Yiannis Papadimitriou, Greek Commercial Counsellor, New York, NY. In addition, I am grateful to Theresa Papademetriou of the Library of Congress, Washington, DC, for always taking the time to help me with my research no matter how small the point in question.

I feel honoured that Gerald Asher agreed to write the introduction, and could hardly have been more pleased. I do not think another writer on wine could better appreciate the task. I am indebted to Julian Jeffs, editor of Faber and Faber's wine series, for his great patience in preparing the manuscript for the printer.

Finally, in another vein altogether, I would like to thank my friends Gary Laden, Jon Nowick, Kevin Lanagan, Marie Winfrey Bernegger, and Hal McNitt for their encouragement. I believe I may rightly call them 'salt and bean friends', from Plutarch's description of 'friends who are so close to us as to be content to dine with us on salt and a bean', although I have never known any of my group to stop there.

Excerpts from the translations of ancient Greek texts are reprinted by permission of The Loeb Classical Library and Harvard University Press.

Foreword

In *The Hill of Kronos*, his autobiographical chronicle of wandering through Greece with a knapsack at various times in his life, Peter Levi, the Oxford classicist and poet, describes an encounter in the 1960s with a priest in a remote village: 'He gave me lunch, an enormous lunch at half past three in the afternoon, fried eggs from [his] Byzantine hens, and a wine that tasted of rocks and bushes.'

With those few words Levi plunges us into a Greek universe where wine is robust and elemental. Made from ancient, indigenous vine varieties, Greek wines were and are prized for their individuality. The character of each is sacred, to be preserved, protected, and, above all, appreciated.

Stavroula Kourakou, the formidable director of the Greek Wine Institute until her recent retirement, began more than twenty years ago a campaign further to protect the originality and quality of Greek wines. In the face of Greek entry into the European Common Market, she proposed and won approval of a system of controlled appellations in which indigenous Greek vine varieties would be matched to those areas in which the best Greek wines had traditionally been produced. At the same time, new standards of viticulture and wine-making were imposed for those appellations to raise quality levels.

It would be perverse to deny the need for the imposition of controlled appellations, because by the 1960s the resin jar had come close to eradicating the distinctions and the quality of Greek wines. This was not because all wines were resinated, but because resin – too conveniently to hand, a veil ready to be drawn over error whenever necessary – had become a disincentive to careful, distinctive wine-making.

Change was wrought with discretion. By enhancing those characteristics that made a Greek wine inherently Greek, a new generation of enologists, though trained mostly in France and Germany, began to uncover one forgotten wine after another, as if removing accumulated grime from a picture and revealing detail that had lain long neglected behind it. I felt this stir of activity when I spent a few days in Athens in the mid-1970s and encountered for the first time, not only the labels of unfamiliar producers, but the names of grape varieties and of entire wine regions I hardly knew existed.

At a dinner in his Alexandria apartment not long after (Alexandria, Virginia, that is, not the city of Athenaeus), Miles Lambert-Gócs let me ramble on before starting to pull from cartons and closets wines from Crete, from Santorini, from Naousa, from Rapsani. Since then, my rediscovery of Greek wine – largely with his help – has been a constant pleasure to me. I might not yet have met Peter Levi's wine, tasting of rocks and bushes, but I have found others, impeccably made, with the stamp of place and time that, in wine, has ever been the hallmark of quality and distinction. Why else do we talk of appellations and vintages?

Lambert-Gócs tempers his enthusiasm with scholarship, writing of Greek wine objectively, while drawing on vast personal experience and relying on his own sure judgment. He tells us that Greek wines, from grape varieties unfamiliar in the West, and produced in distinctive environments, do not lend themselves to comparison with others. But then neither does this book. It is a richly engaging survey of men and wines, of islands, mountains and vineyards, of food and folklore, of past and present. Its pages illuminate brilliantly not only Greek viticulture, but Greece itself.

Gerald Asher
San Francisco
July 1989

Introduction:
Greek Wine in Modern Times

Athenaeus's outstanding third-century AD account of gastronomy in the ancient world, *The Deipnosophists*, provides evidence of the continued production of wine at Greek places famed for wine during antiquity, as that era came to a close. Fragments of information from the Byzantine centuries that followed indicate the further survival of wine-growing at many of the individual locales. Usually the evidence consists of cadastral or tax notations, but sometimes archaeological finds as well, and occasionally even a morsel more palatable to a latter-day Athenaeus, such as the twelfth-century Byzantine poem 'The Abbot's Table', in which the author, Theodoros Prodromos, boasts of having managed four goblets of Khian (Chian) wine, one of the most prized of Aegean vintages during antiquity, and clearly as highly thought of as late as Prodromos's day. Documents from places later ruled by the Venetians, and travelogues of still later Western visitors to the Greece of Ottoman times, attest to more recent perpetuation of the Greek tradition in wine at particular places.

The continuity of wine-growing at the remarkable, environmentally idiosyncratic sites of antiquity would in turn have favoured the retention of previously acclimatized grape varieties, at least in so far as those varieties had not been valued only in conjunction with certain archaic wine-making practices, such as the use of particular flavouring substances, that were discontinued as a result of the technological developments that took place subsequent to the ancient era. In that regard, it ought to be noted that in the earliest record of modern Greek grape varieties, a poem of 1601 (see page 207), the thirty-four varietal names mentioned must have been commonly known for a long time before. Furthermore, they refer to varieties mostly having characteristics typical of vines of the Eastern Mediterranean and Black Sea areas, rather than Western Europe. Nevertheless, in spite of the continuity of Greek wine tradition as tied to place of production, changes between the ancient and modern eras would have taken place following accommodation to wine-making innovations. Most notably, the gradual switch-over from earthenware jars to wooden barrels, which began to occur in Greece sometime after Strabo's seemingly bemused mention of 'wooden jars' being used along Italy's central Adriatic coast in the first century AD, would probably have entailed alterations in practices and occasioned some changes in wine characteristics.

A gradual degradation in Greek wine tradition as concerns quality began in the late Middle Ages, as the Byzantine administration started to deteriorate. Feudalism spread on the Greek mainland, and increasingly obliged the peasants to deliver work and produce to their landlords. Viticulture took on a special importance for the peasants, since it was the one sphere of endeavour in which they were allowed some independence of action, although a tax had to be paid for the privilege. Vineyards could usually be freely created and transferred, and records from some places indicate that peasants often held several vineyard plots, typically dispersed ones, and sometimes even in different villages, their aim being possibly to offset the negative effects of less favourable seasonal conditions on one plot by resort to another. By the early fourteenth century, family economic well-being in parts of the mainland had become so heavily vested in vineyards that fragmentation of holdings brought about by customary law pertaining to inheritance and dowries, as well as by sales of vineyard plots to enable the economic survival of families, added to the impoverishment of the peasantry stemming from other causes. Lack of funds spelled decreased capacity for the input necessary to produce the best wine possible from the vineyards that remained in private possession, while activity by the small category of merchants involved with wine production was generally too limited to counteract the effect of the evolution in landholding patterns.

With the decline of wine quality at the level of peasant production, the best of local wine traditions gradually became concentrated in monastic communities. Monasteries often took over ownership of vineyards which peasants had been forced to sell and in that way also garnered the best vineyard lands. Because of their financial endowments, the religious communities also possessed outstanding facilities for wine-making, remarked upon even centuries later by Western visitors to Greek monasteries:

> The cellar [of the monastery of Mega Spilion, at Kalavryta in the Peloponnesos] was not far off. A large . . . indenture in the cavern, Polypheneus-looking, wide and broad, and particularly lofty, constituted as fine a repository for the purpose as the most numerous community could desire. Huge wine-barrels, of Heidelberg pretensions, lay ranged in imposing order, according to their seniority, which, as we passed along, was carefully noted. The different contributing 'ἀμπέλια' [ambélia], or vineyards, were also duly and variously honoured, as their vintage held a higher or lower place in the estimate of the fraternity.
>
> (Thomas Wyse, *An Excursion in the Peloponnesus*, 1865)

Later, under the Ottomans, the monasteries generally lost their claim on financial resources they possessed at distant places under other jurisdictions, but were granted tax-exempt status.

The Ottoman occupation of the Greek lands began in the fourteenth century, that is, even before the fall of Constantinople (Istanbul) in 1453. In the early centuries of its rule, the Ottoman administration generally made no attempt to curtail wine-growing among the indigenous population. On the contrary, local Ottoman officials, thrown on their own resources to generate income, were usually anxious to protect wine-growing, which could be an outstanding source of revenue if the place concerned were a viable commercial producer and no other more lucrative crop could compete. The number of merchants dealing in wine consequently increased at not a few mainland towns. Furthermore, the lands at the disposal of the Ottoman officials often included vineyards, and the officials might also enjoy the privilege of a monopoly on sales of must to traders – whom they might then proceed to tax – for periods of up to two months after the vintage, thereby assuring themselves premium prices. The Ottomans did not seek to curtail the drinking of wine either, and not only because the infidels' consumption was in the officials' pecuniary interest. The fact is that not all Moslems on Greek territory heeded the Prophet's strictures against wine drinking, especially not converts from Christianity, whose number was by no means negligible in some areas of the mainland and on Crete. Indeed, no Western visitor who spent much time in Ottoman Europe could fail to make humorous note of laxity in that matter:

3

One cadi [Moslem village elder] who was a great *amateur* told me . . . that if Mohammed had known this wine, he would have made a verse expressly to prescribe its usage, the creator not having given such a drink only for the pleasure of Christians.

(François Pouqueville, *Voyage de la Grèce*, 1826)

Negative influences on wine-growing were compounded in the course of the Ottoman centuries, however. The more persistent and deleterious effects emanated from taxation, although even in that respect, the Ottoman system varied from place to place and time to time. On the whole, more accessible places were taxed harder than more remote ones, a circumstance usually favouring the Archipelago, which the Turks generally seem to have avoided as a habitation, and out-of-the-way mountainous places on the mainland. Also, the circumstances under which a place had come under Ottoman control, that is, whether 'voluntarily' or not, was another determining factor, which again usually favoured the islands, since most of them had acquiesced in the takeover because of the impossibility of effective armed resistance. Conversely mountainous places on the mainland sometimes did not acquiesce, but were effectively left 'free' anyway, simply because the resistance they could mount made their molestation not worth the bother from the Ottoman standpoint, provided some token arrangement of overlordship could be worked out. Usually, the Ottoman administrators were content to let previous local custom govern the rate of taxation on wine production, as if deferring to the Byzantine experience as to how much could be extracted without causing the peasants to neglect their vineyards altogether. The local inhabitants, for their part, were most satisfied if the resident Ottoman officials were strangers to their place and customs.

The taxation system began to break down under pressure from a nascent capitalism that grew in mainland towns as from the fifteenth century. The towns attracted inhabitants from the more heavily oppressed countryside, to such an extent that by the end of the eighteenth century the French visitor Félix Beaujour found what he reckoned to be half of arable Macedonia uncultivated. The population shift caused a decline in the revenues of rural Ottoman officials, and spurred them on to heavy tax depredations when the Porte began losing control over its provincial representatives in the eighteenth century. As Ottoman rule began to collapse, both the frequency and cupidity of tax collection grew, and in cases where the tax on wine production was assessed against a village as a whole, a larger assessment on the peasantry had to compensate for the tax-exempt status of monasteries. In the late eighteenth and nineteenth centuries, some local potentates turned very nasty in their dealings with wine-growers. Some were known to prevent the transport of harvested grapes from the vineyards until the arbitrary tax had been paid, thus causing the grapes to deteriorate in the meantime. Or they might turn their animals loose in the vineyards for free grazing, just to show who could exert the really big crush at vintage. In order to complete the vintage as soon as possible, before untoward interference by the authorities, wine-growers found it expedient to gather the fruit of their dispersed parcels of land all at once, irrespective of the state of ripeness of the grapes, to the detriment of wine quality. In a few rare cases (one possible instance is mentioned on page 210), that practice, which has yet to disappear entirely, may have originated in a traditional type of wine deliberately made from a must of under-ripe and over-ripe grapes.

The Ottomans were forced to withdraw piecemeal from Greek territory between 1829 and 1913. As a result of the Greek War of Independence, fought during 1821–9, the Ottomans relinquished somewhat less than half of Greece's present territory, mostly on the southern mainland (Central Greece and the Peloponnesos). Open commercial enterprise thus became possible in free Greece, but wine-growers in most places were in no position to benefit. In a pattern that would be repeated as the rest of Greece was freed, the Ottomans had uprooted or burned vineyards in many places – one Greek reporter of the day noted that the greater part of mainland vineyards suffered that fate – either as part of military operations, or merely as a rearguard reprisal. Even liberated islands, notably among the Cyclades, that were unscathed during the war, and could otherwise have been expected to profit from the new economic climate, were unable to take advantage, since they had expended their financial resources on the struggle for independence. Those areas of Greece that remained under the Turks continued to suffer throughout the decline of Ottoman rule, and in some cases became immersed in increasing violence and warfare that sapped resources of all sorts.

Greek wine-growing took a long time to recover from nearly five centuries of Ottoman occupation. In the decades immediately following the War of Independence, free Greece had little incentive to expand or upgrade commercial wine-making. Towns were rather few and small, and many town-dwellers owned vineyards, or had relatives who did, in their native area, through which they largely kept themselves supplied with wine. Consequently, the domestic market for surplus wine production, though never absent, was limited. Incentive for wine-growers came in the second half of the nineteenth century, but in the form of demand by a Western clientele seeking wine for blending during the pan-European period of vine-yard afflictions. The wine-blending trade sustained interest in viticulture in some areas, but generally encouraged a sacrifice of quality for quantity. In free Greece in particular, the virtually guaranteed market for blending-wine resulted in the expedient planting of currant vines, whose fresh fruit could be vinified if the price proved more attractive, all across the northern Peloponnesos: here the acreage in currants rose from 4,350 hectares in 1878 to 56,400 hectares in 1905, and came to comprise 35 per cent of the vineyards of free Greece.

Greece itself did not escape the diseases and pests that had descended on European vineyards. Phylloxera was by far the most destructive, but its course in Greece was distinguished from all its other manifestations in Europe by the extremely slow rate at which the pest progressed through the country (see the accompanying map). Phylloxera first appeared on the north-eastern mainland and some of the northerly Aegean islands in the late nineteenth century, but in most of Greece it arrived later. Its advance was slowed in some cases by natural barriers – it may be usefully recalled that Greece has ever comprised an assemblage of very distinct geographic units – and in other cases by large gaps in vineyard areas that were occasioned by earlier depopulation and destruction. Some parts of continental Greece were not hit by phylloxera until the 1950s, 1960s, and 1970s; indeed, a large part of the country still remains untouched by the pest. Consequently Greece has had a late recovery from phylloxera, and even where the process of replanting was begun relatively early it was delayed by hostilities, beginning with the Balkan Wars of 1912–13 and ending only with the Greek Civil War of 1947–9, and by emigration, which has plagued numerous Greek wine locales from early in this century until the present day.

For a long time the government of the modern Greek state remained aloof from wine-growing and other such mundane matters, being preoccupied with more central matters of state. The onset of phylloxera, however, forced the Greek government into active involvement. A task force led by the French viticulturalist Pierre Viala was commissioned to report on the phylloxera situation in Greece, and its findings, drafted in 1914, became the basis for setting up a network of government stations to supply new rootstock material to Greek wine-growers. Ampelographic studies were also commissioned. Legislation included the abolishing of taxes on vines, and the halting of the spread of currant vines over the Peloponnesos. When the viability of Greek wine production was generally threatened by world wine gluts during the two decades between the First and Second World Wars, the government urged the establishment of cooperatives, through which growers might join forces and survive. In the island of Samos, for example, the establishment of a cooperative was imposed by the government by legislation of 1934, in order to defuse a highly charged local situation brought about by the gluts.

For most of the twentieth century, Greece's internal underdevelopment and external dependence combined to confine commercial wine-making mostly to bulk sales of blending-wine. Nevertheless, bottled wine gradually gained ground in response to the growth of towns, coming into its own after the Second World War, with the burgeoning of the cities of Athens, Thessaloniki and Patras, and the steady rise in the number of tourists – over 8 million annually in the 1980s – from abroad. The immediate goal in bottled wine generally was the rather modest one of producing stable wines of standardized type, for wide consumption. Although the results were not of the kind to attract international attention, the way was opened to the production of superior bottled wines. The requirements of standardized wine production necessitated the instruction of growers through commercial agents and government agronomists, and made grower follow-through worthwhile financially, while the standardized wines largely broke down lingering Greek consumer resistance to bottled wines, which was in part a legacy of the times when families made and drank their own wine, or that of a relative or special family friend, and did not have confidence in wines sold by just any merchant.

A new plateau in modern Greek wine history was reached in 1969, with the adoption of legislation establishing a national framework for authorizing qualifying wines to bear certain geographic place-names, either in the form of a 'controlled appellation of origin' (*onomasía proeléfseos elenkhoméni*), or an 'appellation of origin of superior quality' (*onomasía proeléfseos anotéras piótitos*)): see page

12 for further explanation of these terms. The step was taken with a view towards Greece's accession to the European Economic Community (EEC), and was therefore designed to conform with the EEC's system of appellative regulation. Legislation of 1971 and 1972 conferred appellation status on certain wines of twenty-one locales, and in the 1980s four further locales were awarded the distinction. The Ministry of Agriculture's Wine Institute (*Institoúton Ínou* [*Oinou*]), founded in 1937, but effectively engaged only since 1952, has been the prime mover in the process of establishing appellative zones, and instrumental as well in formulating the details of the technical requirements (yields per hectare, alcohol content, etc.) to be met by qualifying wines in each recognized zone. The Institute fully expects other appellation zones to be added in coming years, and is currently developing a conceptual framework for inaugurating legislation pertaining to the awarding of *vin de pays*/'country wine' (*topikós ínos* [*oinos*]) status.

At present, the outlook for the future of commercial Greek wine is more favourable than it has been for many centuries. Large private wineries are leading the way in introducing contemporary technology. Cooperative wineries, whose potential in some of the appellation of origin areas is very considerable, are gradually resolving, sometimes with the aid of EEC funding, financial constraints that have held them back from achieving their best in bottled wine. Small individual growers are returning to the Greek bottled-wine market after a long lapse of interest, usually adopting new technology as their resources permit, as well as employing the services of enologists on a seasonal basis. The results of these developments are to be seen in new bottled wines that have appeared in Greece with increased frequency since the mid-1970s. Quality may not as yet be representative of the best traditions of the places concerned in each instance, but the varied work of the Wine Institute is devoted to determining the precise conditions for high-quality wine at the various locales, and to balancing the best in local traditions with the demands of the world market. Throughout the spectrum of the Greek wine industry it is fervently believed that in achieving that balance Greece will in the twenty-first century regain the reputation in wine it first earned in ancient times.

NOTES ON GAINING FAMILIARITY WITH GREEK WINE

Greece remains the most difficult of wine countries to become acquainted with, and its wines continue to confound enophiles. One would like to see a concerted effort on the part of the Greek industry – large firms, cooperatives, small private producers – to improve the situation, but they remain hamstrung by jealousies, mutual suspicions and secretiveness that recall the ancients, at their worst, and inhibit action for the common good. In these circumstances, non-Greeks are left largely on their own, and how they fare is too often utterly a matter of chance, all of which may be in order according to the eternal Greek way of thinking, but not infrequently damaging for the reputation of Greek wine.

Somewhat stagnant economic conditions mean that numerous noteworthy or even outstanding Greek wine-growing areas remain confined to artisanal production, entirely outside the sphere of bottling. One must sometimes spend days at such places in order to comprehend the nature, logic and worthiness of the sounder of their traditions and practices in wine-making. As for bottled Greek wines, one ought to be aware that few of the better ones have been exported at all, even fewer are exported on an ongoing basis, and still fewer are ever distributed abroad outside Greek ethnic channels. Bottled wines of limited production can be difficult to locate even in Greece.

Nor, as yet, does satisfaction necessarily follow upon finding a Greek wine that one has sought out, unless one is lucky enough to have the opportunity of meeting Greeks who own a home cellar – their number has been multiplying in recent years with improvements in income and living standards. In Greek retail shops and restaurants, however, one will not encounter bottles of cellarable wine that have been laid down for several years, and so the wine may not be 'ready'. Furthermore, storage facilities in commercial establishments are rarely of the standard required for a successful outcome in laying wine aside for improvement in bottle. Indeed storage conditions generally are so poor in retail shops that even a well-made wine may sometimes embarrass its producers through no fault of theirs. Nevertheless, in Athens and at some of the major resort areas there are shops where wines may be bought with a good deal of confidence. Major supermarket chains have also become most reliable sources of supply, and are stocking a more than adequate variety, sometimes including limited-production wines.

The customer buying Greek wine can usually ensure avoiding an unhappy purchase by one means or another. For example, many Greek wines are still put in clear glass bottles, and can be examined for signs of brownish colour, which in all but a few instances indicates a deteriorated condition. Also, vintage dates are increasingly appearing on Greek wines of quality; by law, Greek wines with a vintage indication must be produced from the specified vintage in an amount of at least 85 per cent. In the case of appellation of origin wines, whether or not vintage-dated, a Ministry of Agriculture banderole across the mouth of the bottle will display the last two digits of the year the bottle was released from the winery, behind the slash after the initials of the appellation region. For vintage-dated appellation wines, any overage between the release date and the maturation times mentioned in this book for specific wines may be taken to represent time spent in bottle at the winery. In the case of wines from cooperatives, it is often desirable that any such discrepancy should be minimal, since their capacity for safely storing bottles is typically not up to accommodating production volume. It still happens that cooperatives will release a once satisfying wine on to the market when it is already at the upper limit of its qualitative potential, with the result that some bottles start going flat in a short time. An ocean voyage can cause them to arrive in that condition on overseas markets, where the reputation of Greek wine can hardly afford such occurrences. More prudent stock management will necessarily be part of the solution.

On the other hand, one can shift too much of the onus of responsibility for ensuring satisfaction with Greek wine on to the wines themselves. Sometimes that tendency takes the form of holding contemporary Greek wines to an exaggerated standard derived from the ancient record. At other times, irrelevant foreign models are imposed as the standard of quality. In the latter regard, it ought to be kept in mind that Greek wines are typically the products of distinctive environments and grape varieties unfamiliar to Western enophiles. Consequently, the colours, bouquets and flavours of Greek wines – and not least in the very best of them – for the most part do not lend themselves to direct comparison with wines of other more familiar, and perhaps more popular, places. Familiarity with Greek wine therefore demands an extra fund of experience, including such matters as cellaring time and serving temperature, in addition to all the other factors more directly pertaining to wine appreciation.

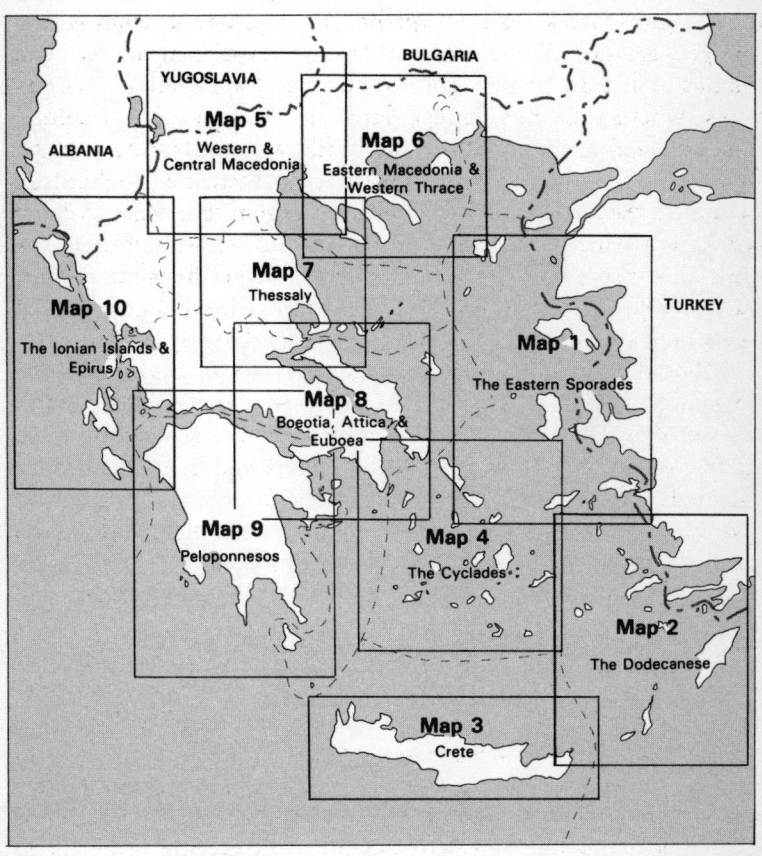

Greek Appellations of Origin

The Greek appellation of origin system is meant to ensure that wines bearing the stated appellation have been made in accordance with sound regional practice for the production of quality wine. An appellation regulation requires the use of choice grape varieties, delineates the areas having appropriate soils for the production of quality wine from those varieties, specifies the system of cultivation, and sets a maximum level of vine yields and a minimum level of sugar content in the grape must. Additionally, in the case of 'controlled' appellations of origin, more detailed reporting as regards such matters as varietal composition of vineyards, vine age, new plantings, and quantities of wines made and in stock is required, in order to monitor development of the region itself. Thus far, the 'controlled appellation' system has been applied only to liqueur wines. The appellation system is administered by the Central Committee for the Protection of Wine Production (KEPO), under the Ministry of Agriculture. It should be noted, however, that the appellation system is not meant as a guarantee of the quality of a particular wine.

To date, the following appellations of origin have been authorized. Wines authorized to bear an appellation of origin are issued numbered banderoles that must be affixed over the mouth of each bottle. In the case of a 'controlled appellation of origin', the banderole is blue and white; in the case of a 'appellation of origin of superior quality', the banderole is red and white. The appellation initials, as they appear on the banderoles, are noted in parentheses below.

Controlled Appellations of Origin (*Onomasía Proeléfseos Elenkhoméni*)

Mavrodaphne of Cephalonia (MK)

Mavrodaphne of Patras (MΠ)

Muscat of Cephalonia (MK)

Muscat of Limnos (ΛM)

Muscat of Patras (MΠ)

Muscat of Rhodes (MP)

Muscat of Rion of Patras (MP)

Samos (*ΣM*)

Appellations of Origin of Superior Quality (*Onomasía Proeléfseos Anotéras Piótitos*)

Amyntaion (AM)	Limnos (ΛM)	Playies Melitona (ΠM)
Ankhialos (AX)	Mantinia (MN)	Peza (ΠZ)
Arkhanes (AP)	Naousa (NΣ)	Rapsani (PΨ)
Dafnes (ΔΦ)	Nemea (NM)	Rhodes (PΔ)
Goumenissa (ΓM)	Paros (ΠP)	Robola of Cephalonia (PK)
Kantza (KN)	Patras (ΠT)	Santorini (ΣN)
		Sitia (ΣT)

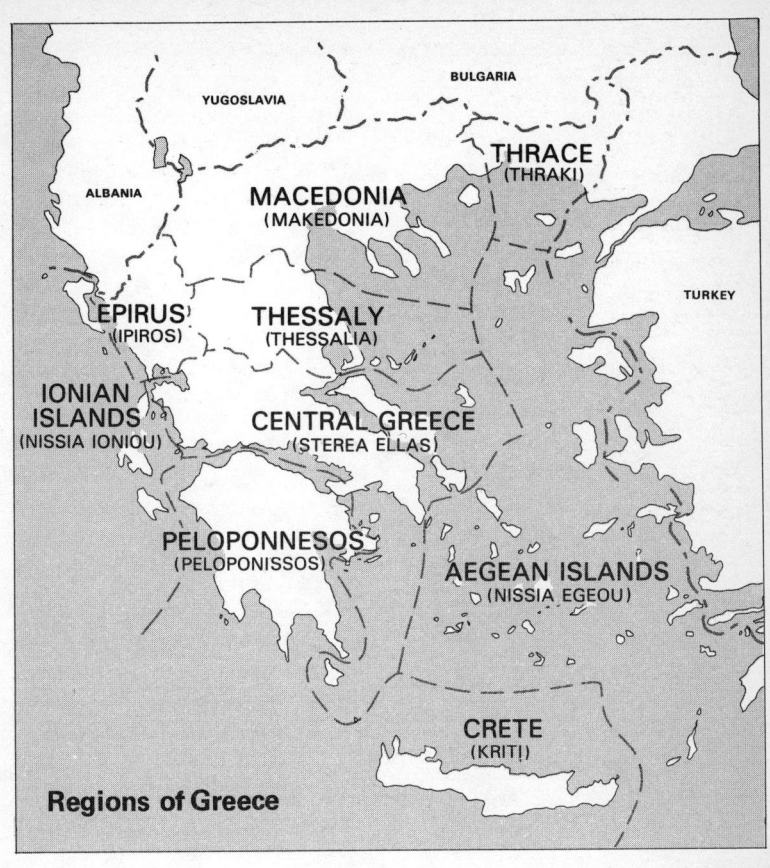

Regions of Greece

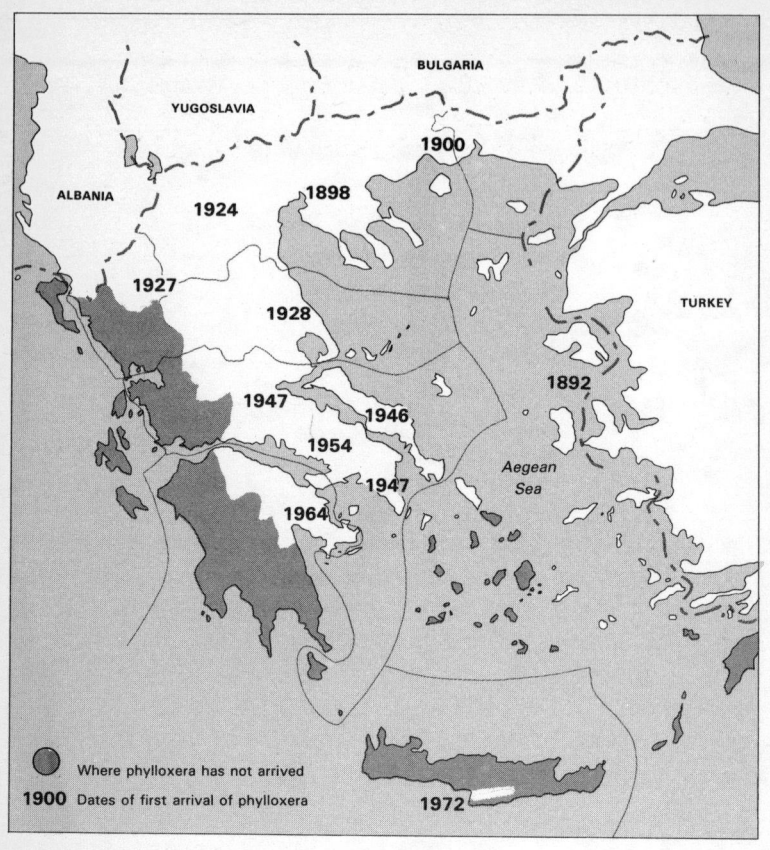

PART I
THE AEGEAN ISLANDS

I

Samos and the Eastern Sporades

———

The wines [of Samos] are in large part muscats and more white than red. Far from meriting the reproaches which were formerly addressed to them . . . by Strabo and Apuleius, they are, on the contrary, now justly renowned among all those of the Archipelago, and if they are not deserving of being placed in the first rank, they can occupy the second without much handicap.
(Victor Guérin, French traveller, *Description de l'île de Patmos et de l'île de Samos*, 1856)

SAMOS

By far the most widely known place-name in Greek wine over the past several centuries has been Samos. Samos is a lofty island – its very name is thought to come from the Phoenician word for 'heights' – lying just off the mainland of Asia Minor, in the east-central Aegean. Early Aegean wine-growers observed that superior elevation tends to aid wine quality, which may explain why Samos sported vineyards even in times before it became a centre of the Ionian civilization spawned along the littoral. None the less, the ancients would doubtless be surprised by Samos's recent success with wine. In their era, Samian wines ranked far below a host of other Aegean wines, while the geographer Strabo stated that everything grown on Samos *except* wine was of excellent quality. The discrepancy in opinion between ancient and modern times is not attributable to a deterioration in quality standards or a change in taste generally, but to a shift in Samiote wine tradition which occurred during the intervening centuries.

One detects in Strabo's mention of Samos's felicitous environment for agriculture some surprise as to why only the grape-vine should be so disfavoured. Later history indicates the reason to have been

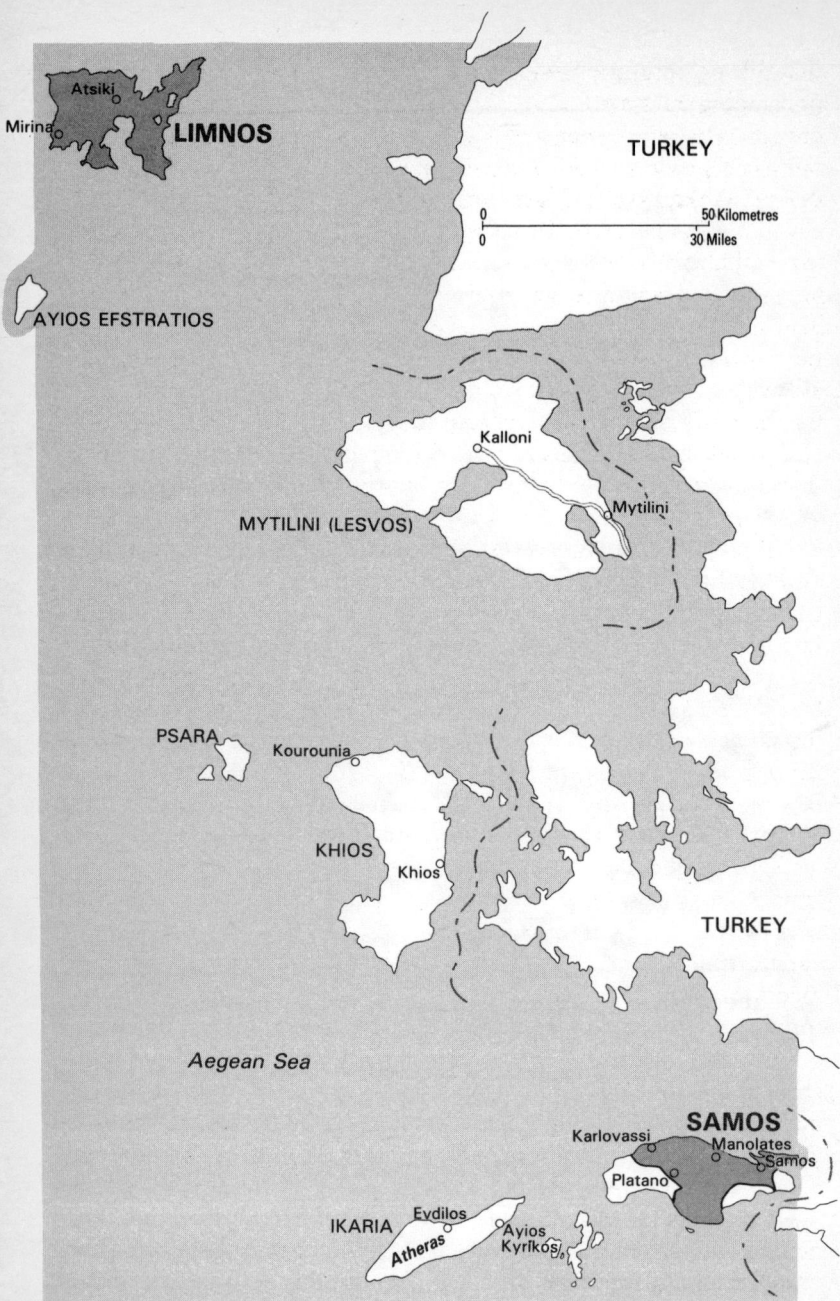

The Eastern Sporades

that during antiquity Samos did not acquire grape varieties capable of bringing out its potential for viticulture. Right up to the fifteenth century AD, Samos seems to have been known in the Greek world only as a producer and trader of red wine, and that was probably dry rather than sweet. The retreat of the red began fortuitously with a near depopulation of the island that occurred around 1475, when most inhabitants departed for Khios after several decades of constant harassment by pirates seeking refuge on Samos's wooded shores. Towards the end of the sixteenth century, piracy began to abate, and the Ottoman sultan offered privileges, including land grants, tax alleviations and a measure of home rule, to encourage resettlement. By the early seventeenth century, Samos was once again densely populated. Its vineyards were flourishing too, but with the difference that the variety called *moskháto áspro* (white muscat), or just *moskháto*, had become characteristic of the island.

The *moskháto áspro* is so widespread in Greece, especially insular Greece, that it must almost certainly have been grown in the Aegean islands during antiquity. Some classicists have regarded the varietal family described in Latin as *apiana* by Pliny in his *Natural History* to have been the muscats, primarily because the name signified that bees (*apis*) liked it, much as the modern name *muscatello* may indicate the same about flies (*musca*). Although *muscatello* was more likely derived from the Greek term *moskháto*, and therefore from the Persian term *moushk* (musk), the possibility of a muscat/*apiana* identity nevertheless merits consideration, since the *apiana* varieties were associated with sweet wines. Pliny stated that those wines had 'a peculiar flavour which is not that of wine', by which he may have been alluding to the characteristic muscat scent that causes the varietal family to be termed 'aromatic'. We might note here his mention of the fact that the Greeks called *apiana* vines 'psithian' (*psíthios*). The word 'psithian' probably came from the name for wormwood, or *apsínthion*, a plant valued for its special aromatic character – and therefore sometimes used as a perfume in wine-making – different though that character is from the scent of muscat grapes. Or does the *psíthios* name therefore refute the identity of the *apiana* and the muscats?

Greek ampelographers think that the *moskháto áspro* originated in Asia Minor, but there is no record of the *moskháto áspro* on Samos until the late sixteenth century, and the island is not known to have been associated with 'psithian' wine during antiquity. Possibly first introduced only during the resettlement, the *moskháto áspro* gained predominance on Samos as the export of muscat wine increased. By the time Joseph Georgirenes wrote the first modern description of Samos, in 1678, the trade in muscat was quite brisk. That commercial success inevitably caused other grape varieties to recede in importance. Nevertheless, red Samian wine continued to be produced in considerable quantity for over two centuries more, as borne out by visitors' reports, and remained a typical island wine until it was dealt a sudden and serious setback during a second replanting of Samos, which followed the arrival of phylloxera in 1892. The island's trade in muscat had thrived while Western Europe's vineyards were recovering from the effects of the pest, and consequently Samian growers thought their future very largely dependent on muscat.

The primacy of the *moskháto áspro* was secured in 1934. At that time, national legislation presaging the later appellation of origin framework was enacted to protect Samian wine-growing, and provided that only the *moskháto áspro* could be used for wine entitled to bear the Samos name commercially. The Union of Vinicultural Cooperatives of Samos (EOSS), was also set up and put under obligation to buy all muscat grapes offered. By thus rendering superfluous any function red wine might have had as a financial cushion in periods of slow sales of muscat, and in effect transferring that advantage to muscat grapes, the legislation effectively banished most of the dark-skinned varieties from the island vineyards, in favour of the more profitable and secure *moskháto*. Today, of the approximately 2,000 hectares of vineyards on Samos, or nearly one-tenth of the cultivated area, about 95 per cent is planted in that variety.

The legislation of 1934 was motivated by the Greek government's desire to bring a halt to deteriorating economic and social conditions on Samos. A world wine glut had taken its toll on grower income, prompting wine-growers to form an organization to protect their interests *vis-à-vis* the more than two dozen wine traders on Samos, who had organized themselves into a union. The two groups cooperated for a time and made contractual arrangements, but as the world market continued to deteriorate the traders' union discontinued contracting and the organization of growers responded by marketing their product on their own, underselling the traders. A great deal of antagonism was fomented on Samos, growers on the one side, and traders and their employees on the other. Further, the very low prices asked by the growers' organization reduced foreign exchange earnings, and threatened the reputation of Samian wine.

To forestall violence and prevent lasting damage, the Greek government ultimately stepped in to reorder the commercial framework of wine-growing on Samos. The production and trade functions for Samian wine were fused in one organization, EOSS, which has no counterpart elsewhere in Greece. It is an 'obligatory' system of cooperatives, whereby growers must sell all of their grapes to EOSS, except for amounts allowed for household use, while the Union, for its part, is obliged to purchase all grapes offered to it by growers. Furthermore, EOSS has exclusive authority to produce Samian wine for commercial sale, although it may sell wine to other, off-island bottlers for marketing under their own label, with the Samos appellation, if the wine qualifies.

Given its 'obligatory' nature, EOSS has to contend with a certain added threat to wine quality. To ward off the potential negative effects of the system in that respect, various measures are taken, beginning with a detailed specification of where vines may and may not be planted. Moreover, no increase in the total authorized area will be permitted. The vineyards of Samos are located in most parts of the island, but mainly on the northern side between the ports of Karlovassi and Samos, respectively on the west and east, where EOSS has its two wineries. Variation in elevation is considerable, ranging from practically sea level at some points to 800 metres above it. Soil varies in chemical consistency, but is pebbly, calcareous, and well drained at most vineyard sites. The intense insolation everywhere is tempered by sea breezes, which blow so strongly that short pruning of the vines is required, if sporadically at the risk of some rotting when grape clusters brush the ground (the latter condition, by the way, was apparently that in which bees preferred to have *apiana* grapes, if *apiana* was indeed muscat). Having observed the performance of Samos's vineyards for decades, EOSS has a decided view as to the very best vineyard areas, most of which are found in the semi-mountainous zone. But while it would like to take advantage of its experience in that regard, to produce even single vineyard wines, commercial demand generally has not warranted EOSS's moving in that direction.

Owing to the variation in vineyard exposure and altitude, grapes are delivered to EOSS between July and September, and sometimes into October from the terraces at higher altitudes. A year's output of must usually falls between 80,000 and 100,000 hectolitres, though even in the eastern Aegean an exceptionally poor vintage can occur. In processing the raw material, EOSS employs several means to reserve the best Samian grapes for sweet wine. Between 6 and 10 per cent of a year's must is required to be distilled, and quantities of must, as well as industrial wine for vermouth, are exported. EOSS also makes its own vermouth. Furthermore, about one-quarter of the must is vinified for dry wine for bottled sales. As a result of those measures, only about three-fifths of a year's must goes to produce sweet muscat wines. A further stipulation protecting wine quality, as well as ensuring authenticity, is that Samos is closed to the landing of must or wine in barrel. Yet the most direct and important factor in maintaining the quality of Samos's sweet muscat wine is the observance of the traditional differentiation among the island's several varieties of it.

In recommending in an article of 1914 that Samian wine production should be converted to a cooperative basis, the Greek agronomist G. Palamiotis expressed his concern that under the marketing pressures of the day the operations of the island's private traders would result in the loss of the Samian tradition in wine-making. He was particularly disturbed that at that time almost no sweet muscat wine was being produced commercially. What was exported as Samos Muscat was actually mistelle, unfermented must to which grape spirits are added. Alcohol content was simply brought to 12–15° by the addition, leaving sugar concentration at about 230–60 grams per litre. Traditionally, Samian sweet muscat wine was produced by any of four methods, all involving fermentation, and resulting in five individual types of wine. Palamiotis believed that the Samian tradition of muscat was in the best long-run interest of all the island's inhabitants, and today EOSS is maintaining the variety at the heart of that tradition.

Un-Aged Sweet Wines from Fresh Grapes

Two kinds of Samos muscat wine are made from fresh grapes harvested at peak maturation. The grapes may come from any area of the island authorized for *moskháto áspro*, as long as their must attains a minimum sugar content of 260 grams per litre. Both wines are ready for bottling within months of the vintage. They are of a deep golden colour, and while they exhibit 'only' varietal aroma, it can be of such penetrating and quintessentially muscat quality that one might be excused for musing about the *apiana*/muscat question and recalling that Columella (*De Re Rustica*) included *apiana* with the vines 'most renowned for their precious flavours', even if Pliny described these as somewhat 'peculiar' for wine.

SAMOS GLYKO (OR SAMOS DOUX)

The major wine of Samos, and the one that originally formed the basis of Samos's trade in wine after the repopulation, is a kind produced by crushing the grapes, removing the skins immediately, and arresting fermentation with grape spirits of 95–96° once fermentation has brought natural sugar content down to 160 grams per litre. Alcohol is left at 13.5°. It was fortification and stabilization of that sort that made it feasible to ship wine of Glyko type far and wide in earlier centuries. It was surely the sort of Samian wine that the wine writer André Jullien had in mind in 1816 when he assigned Samos to his third rank of wines.

The bright colour and intense, spiced apricot aroma of Samos Glyko attract people to it like flies, but some are afterwards put off by its rather unctuous texture, and are unable to get beyond the initial flavour, as the wine livens up. Others dislike the aromatic flavour, which is virtually the same as that of Samian muscat grapes; I must suppose they would not enjoy those either. Perhaps a few others are put off by the fact that such plainly good sweet wine should be so affordably available. Still others, however, never stop going back for more of it throughout their years of wine drinking, even after they have become acquainted with dessert wines – not the least of which may also be Samian – that they might concede to be better in certain respects. For the faithful, only the words of Marguerite Yourcenar adequately capture the virtues of Samos Glyko:

> a cup of Samos drunk at noon in the heat of the sun or, on the contrary, absorbed of a winter evening when fatigue makes the warm current be felt at once in the hollow of the diaphragm and the sure and burning dispersion spreads along our arteries, such a drink provides a sensation which is almost sacred, and is sometimes too strong for the human head. No feeling so pure comes from

the vintage-numbered cellars of Rome; the pedantry of great connoisseurs of wine wearies me.

(*Memoirs of Hadrian*, 1962)

SAMOS IMIGLYKO (OR SAMOS DEMI-DOUX)

Grapes from the same vineyards and with the same composition as for Samos Glyko are used to produce a must that undergoes a natural fermentation, that is, one which comes to a halt without the introduction of grape spirits, the traditional method used by islanders who make sweet wine for themselves. The skins are left in the must for the first forty hours of fermentation, so that aroma will be sufficient for what is appropriate to Samos Muscat wine. Longer contact with the skins poses the risk of the wine contracting tannins and related substances that would have a negative influence on flavour; that problem can sometimes be encountered in home-made wines. The colour and aromatic features of Samos Imiglyko are virtually identical to those of Samos Glyko, but at 15° alcohol and only about 55 grams of sugar per litre, divergence in the feel of the wine is to be expected. In particular, it is less unctuous in texture.

In 1982 EOSS began producing a special Imiglyko on commercial order from abroad. A quantity of it was also put out to celebrate the fiftieth anniversary of EOSS in 1984. Called Grands Crus Imiglyko, it is produced from selected grapes from areas known for superior quality. Its advantage over standard Samos Imiglyko is marked in the persistence of its aromatic flavour. Would there were the economic incentive for EOSS to do more along this line!

Aged Sweet Wines from Partially Dried Grapes

Other sweet muscat wines are produced on Samos from selected over-ripened grapes, or from fully ripened ones that have been spread in the sun for seven to eight days following picking; without trying to influence the course of debate over the possibility of an *apiana*/muscat identity, it might be noted, by way of demonstrating that the Greeks have a long habit of doing so with grapes of 'peculiar' character, that Pliny specifically associated 'psithian' wine with raisin wines. In an average year, about 10 per cent of the Samian grape harvest is destined for concentration of sweetness by those methods. The resultant wines are given a more or less lengthy maturation in oak, and can be readily distinguished from Samos Glyko and Samos Imiglyko by their darker colours, which overlap orange and brown, and even hint at reddishness in the ultimate instance. They are also distinguishable by their developed bouquet. It was certainly his acquaintance with at least one of these wines that caused Guérin to challenge Jullien's rating of Samos Muscat; that Jullien did not know of them is clear from his statement that Samian wines would be better 'if they were kept'. Those who wish to drink aged Samian sweet wine, or to put some away for maturation in bottle, should choose from among the following wines, rather than lay down bottles of Samos Glyko or Samos Imiglyko, neither of which has anything to gain from bottle-aging.

SAMOS ANTHEMIS

Apparently known to Guérin, this sort of wine was referred to by him as *anthosmie*, the gallicized rendering of Greek *anthosmía*, or 'flower-smell', that is, 'bouquet'. The term, rather than the particular type of wine, dates back to the ancient Greeks, who applied it generally to the smell of sound older wines, and also had a wine which they produced by a particular technique and called *anthosmías*. EOSS has in this case altered the name for marketing purposes, while otherwise leaving the tradition of Samian *anthosmía* intact. Samos Anthemis is fortified, with grape spirits being added to stop fermentation at about 140 grams of sugar per litre, while alcohol is brought to 15°. It is then matured in oak for three to four years before being bottled, picking up its *anthosmía* in the meantime ('Now even uncompounded substances have certain odours, which men endeavour to assist by artificial means, even as they assist nature in producing palatable tastes': Theophrastus, *Concerning Odours*).

Samos Anthemis offers a smooth gradation of colour from amberish-orange and brown at the centre, to a honey-coloured gold, to a yellowish-gold, and finally to a greenish-yellow at the rim. The greenishness is nascent even further inward, as is true of the orange heading outward. Of course, with accumulated bottle-age, the amber tendency deepens and becomes quite dominant. Anthemis projects a bouquet typical of Samos Glyko, but overlaid by a toasty, slightly toffee-like aroma that becomes more apparent in the mouth. Sweetness and acidity are integrated, forestalling any cloying impression in the course of a mouthful. A vaguely astringent sensation chimes in to enhance the wine's long, firm finish on the tongue.

SAMOS NECTAR

As Glyko is paralleled by Anthemis in being fortified, so Imiglyko is paralleled by Samos Nectar in being the product of a natural fermentation. Since the sugar content of the must in this case is quite elevated, at 500 grams per litre, the fermentation is the most difficult one undergone by any Samian wine, and lasts about three months. Fermentation stops when sugar is at about 100 grams per litre and alcohol at 14–15°. The wine is then aged in oak for four to five years prior to bottling, making it quite unusual among unfortified muscats.

Samos Nectar is of a lustrous orangish colour, and distinguishes itself among muscat wines by the finesse with which it presents the sensations of a very considerable fatness. Its nose might be thought of as an extension of that found on Samos Glyko: there is apricot dominating, but it is now the concentrated essence of it, as in the dried fruit, while smells related to butterscotch also participate. In the mouth, the wine is so concentrated aromatically that the mouth-coating sweetness which keeps aroma pouring out is actually masked in part by it. The aromatic flavour is so intense and persistent that I have never been able to notice any particular sharpness in feel, although as in any wine, it must be a high decree of acidity, intertwined with alcohol and the rest, that provides the backbone to allay any cloying feel. ('This is heaven, let me tell you, and, as I said just now, our drink is nectar': Zeus, in Lucian's *Dialogues of the Gods*.)

PALAIO NECTAR

Writing in 1813, the English visitor John Galt intimated that Samian sweet wines of very advanced age were to be had on the island. Perhaps they were an inadvertent offshoot of early wine gluts, such as the one Galt mentioned. EOSS produces a wine called Palaio Nectar (Old Nectar) by setting aside exceptional wine of Nectar type for additional maturation in barrel, for eight to ten years altogether. By then, Palaio Nectar acquires an almost pinkish shading over a yellowish-brown base, and a dominance of toffee-like smells in bouquet and aromatic flavour. Ordinarily, it would perhaps not be preferred over Samos Nectar, or even the other Samian sweet wines, but Palaio Nectar does stand as something of a rebuke to challengers of Samos, no other unfortified *moskháto áspro* wines having proved up to bearing the sort of maturation it receives without loss of their essential character as muscat wine. Although it is not a commercial wine at present, a bottle of Palaio Nectar is not impossible to acquire from EOSS.

When Byron called for Samian wine, he no doubt had sweet muscat in mind, for this was what Samos generally exported to Athens, where the bard placed his order. A bowl of it might seem a tall order in these calorie-conscious times, and I would therefore suggest a mere glass of it, to be taken at times other than at the conclusion of a major Levantine meal. The middle of a lazy afternoon is a perfect moment, for example.

I am prepared to accept that Samos Glyko is not the wine for everyone. Corresponding in a liquid way to *baklavá* and other such sweet pastries, Glyko might still stir in some of us that very abhorrence *baklavá* once did in Western visitors to the Balkans and beyond:

> There before us, on the table, was a large Baklava cake, compounded of wafer-like paste fried in oil, drenched in syrup, interleaved with walnut mash, and crowned with cream. It was a climax of sweetness, stickiness, oiliness, and indigestibility, and we stood before it struck dumb with horror and surfeit.
>
> (Jan and Cora Gordon, *Two Vagabonds in Albania*, 1927)

Having witnessed in my own time, however, the widespread acceptance of *baklavá* by Westerners, some of whom even have the temerity to distinguish 'better' from 'good', I think there might be some reason to expect that most of us potentially can fathom the harmonies of Samos Glyko. And for those who do, my first recommendation for accompanying it will always be . . . *baklavá*! In the middle of a lazy afternoon, to be sure. That sweet, whether or not 'crowned with cream', is one of those with which we are told no wine can cope, much less agree, yet there is Samos Glyko to do both, and in both the aromatic and tactile spheres of flavour sensation. I would also like to mention how good I have found Glyko with French toast dusted with cinnamon and drizzled with maple syrup. I would drink Samos Imiglyko in quite the same way as I would Glyko, but with less sweet things, such as *finíkia* cookies. If I had my choice, I would take Samos Nectar with *galaktoboúreko* and with creams flavoured with vanilla or caramel, such as *crème caramel*. I find that Samos Anthemis tolerates sharper flavours in desserts than do its brethren: both Anthemis and Palaio Nectar seem to me to offer some resistance to chocolate. However, the thing to do with Palaio Nectar in EOSS's view seems to be to dunk *friganiés* in it, at least in mid-morning. *Friganiés* are browned, oven-dried slices of bread, and the stranger reluctant to join in this use of the vinous rarity might encourage himself by reviewing Athenaeus's long discussion of breads, wherein he mentions a 'brazier bread' (*eskharítin*) intended to be 'dipped in sweet wine', and thus softened before eating.

Samiotes, by the way, urge a bowl of sweet muscat as a morning tonic. I could think their motive base, what with their stocks of muscat wine, but Athenaeus's quotation from Epicharinus's *The Sirens* suggests a very old tradition that is possibly still at work: 'Early in the morning, with the first coming of dawn, we would put on the fire some plump small fry, the roasted flesh of a pig, and some polyps; then we would wash them all down with sweet wine.' Having given the experience several trials, I might say that twentieth-century technological man is sorely in need of the habit. More soberly, I would not recommend more than a decilitre to any but those who are either at their leisure, or else unusually enthusiastic about their employment. Even in that case, however, Epicharinus's suggestion of a bed of food for the wine to fall into upon the drinkers rising from theirs is well worth following ('We at least, belonging neither to the class of those who drink too much nor to those who get drunk in the morning, resort to these erudite symposia': Athenaeus, *The Deipnosophists*).

I should conclude my advice for visitors to Samos first of all by assuring them that the Samiotes do not loll about all day sipping sweet wine in between frolicking on the beach. Actually, one rarely sees a Samiote wine-grower there: 'They bathe only in their own sweat,' a local joked when I naively suggested the non-income benefits of existence as a Samiote grape-grower. In the island villages, people mostly drink resinated dry muscat of their own making, a habit that was introduced on Samos at least as early as the repopulation, when people from the southern mainland, those real heirs to resination, came to settle. A grower up in the village of Platano, one of the island's superb vineyard locales, says he resinates because the wine then seems less sweet (*glykó*), and he prefers it this way as a mealtime beverage. Be that as it may, the joining of muscat aroma with pininess is frowned on by Greek enologists, because the varietal aroma is thus neutralized. Nevertheless, even EOSS makes and bottles its Retsina, which has a good market on Samos and other islands of the eastern Aegean. More *un*resinated dry muscat is made, though. It sells under the Samena label, which can be either 'white' or 'black', denoting respectively the better and the lesser. Both are at 12–13°. White-label Samena would probably qualify for appellation of origin status, were the Samos entitlement extended to dry muscats. However, that step is unlikely because the Greek government fears it would result in a cutback in the production of the ultimately more lucrative, though more slowly sold off, sweet wines.

EOSS also offer a rosé wine called Fokianos, a 12° wine made from the red grape of that name. The *fokianós* carries the name of the ancient Ionian (Asia Minor) city of Phocaea, and is a relic of bygone centuries when Samos made red wines. It occupies nearly the entire 5 per cent of Samos's vineyard land that is not planted with *moskháto áspro*. Assuming that Samian red wine was indeed 'nothing much', the goodness of Fokianos rosé may come as a surprise.

THE EASTERN SPORADES

Samos can be loosely grouped geographically with the rather far-flung islands of the north-eastern Aegean, which are sometimes called the Eastern Sporades. Most of these islands are relatively large and have histories telling of exceptional suitability for vine cultivation in some areas. The only island in the group that at present has any significance in wine, however, is Limnos, the most northerly. An island of low topographic profile, Limnos has its vineyards primarily alongside the shallow valleys of its north-western hill country, extending west from around Atsikí. About 1,000 hectares are planted, of which nearly 700 are in *moskháto alexandrías* (muscat of Alexandria), a variety not generally esteemed for wine-making, but which succeeds unusually well on Limnos and has therefore been entitled to an appellation of origin since 1971. Unlike the case of Samos, both sweet and dry Limniote muscats may qualify for the appellation, and both are produced by the Union of Agricultural Cooperatives of Limnos, the only bottler on the island. The sweet muscat, which is similar to Samos Glyko in flavour and quality, though with more of an alcohol smack it has seemed to me, is usually produced as a fortified wine of 15° alcohol, but may also be found unfortified.

As at Samos, red wine was the dominant type of wine on Limnos in the past. Several Western visitors in recent centuries remarked on finding good dark reds there. However, the profitability of Limniote muscat wine occasioned the spread of the *moskháto alexandrías* subsequent to phylloxera, at the expense of interest in other varieties. The big loser was the indigenous *limnió* – also called *kalabáki* locally – which is the ancient *limnía* variety mentioned by Polydeuctes in the second century AD. The Union bottles an attractive, bright-coloured, light dry red wine from *limnió*, which, like its other wines, is marketed under the Limnos label.

Sizeable Mytilini (Lesvos), south-east of Limnos, grows mostly *limnió*, though no longer in any great quantity. It may be our loss, for in 1553 Pierre Belon advised that Mytilini's wines 'were reputedly the best in the Aegean' at the time. William Turner reported in 1820 that the island's 'black wine [has] some body and a sweet taste, but not enough to be disagreeable'. The semi-sweet red wine of the medieval village of Kalloni retains a particular reputation for excellence, but is made from the black *kalloniátiko* variety. I have found no mention of this variety in Greek ampelographies, which leads me to wonder whether the *kalloniátiko* may actually be a more widely planted Aegean variety generally known by another name, but so-called on Mytilini because there it is planted mostly at Kalloni.

One of the Eastern Sporades of outstanding historical interest is Khios (Chios), directly south of Mytilini. It is with the past foremost in mind, too, with regard to wine, that one has to go there, since nowadays less than 1,000 hectolitres are produced in a year's vintage on all of this sizeable island. The wine pilgrim's destination is in the upper north-western part of Khios, between the Pelinaion and Amoni mountains, in the vicinity of the contemporary villages of Kourounia, Nenitouria and Keramos. It is a rugged and calcareous area, and one subject to somewhat peculiar climatic influences due to the particularly high elevations on its eastward side, together with Khios's broadside position *vis-à-vis* the mainland of Asia Minor just further east. Pausanias related that the island's name comes from the Greek for snow, and an elderly native living in New York has told me of winters in north-western Khios in his youth when sheep lay dead all about, frozen in snow that reached to a man's thighs. This curious area was formerly known as Ariousia, a name that is one of the most illustrious in the annals of wine. For 1500 years its name rang in the ears of Aegean enophiles much as Bordeaux has in ours for the past 150.

Accounts given by numerous Western visitors stopping at Khios between the sixteenth and nineteenth centuries suggest that the tradition of Ariousian wine had remained intact until then, if at a depressed level of production in later years. In 1822, however, the Ottomans effectively laid waste to Khios – as commemorated in words by Victor Hugo and pictures by Delacroix – in retaliation for the Greek uprising of 1821. They wantonly destroyed the vineyards of Ariousia, completing the work of their previous attempt on them at the beginning of the eighteenth century, which had already cut back the region's wine trade. Without a widespread sprinkling of apprised and caring wine lovers who could provide financial support, few vineyards were replanted, and such little recovery as was achieved was practically wiped out by phylloxera and emigration in the early twentieth century. The remnants of Ariousia, such as they are, consist of the paltry 10 hectares of vineyards scattered from 50 to 500 metres above the Aegean at Kourounia, where hundreds of hectares of vines once crowded these steeply inclined slopes. Gone, too, is the name *Arioúsios ínos (oinos)*. Now it is Kourounia, named for the pigs *(gouroúnia)* once raised in numbers thereabouts, that gives its name to the wine, *kourouniótiko krasí*. Still, it appears that there is a lick of the Ariousian tradition left.

Athenaeus mentioned 'three kinds of [Ariousian wine]: one dry, another rather sweet; the third, a mean between these two in taste'. *Kourouniótiko* comes in two kinds: one is a dry *rozé* (rosé), made like a red wine, but from the lightly coloured *rozakiá, soultaní* and *bigléri* grapes, plus the darker *ayianítes* (or *ayianiótiko*); the other is a rather sweet *mávro* (black) made from the grape called by the simple but most venerable name *krasostáfylo* (wine grape), which according to what I have been able to learn is apparently the widespread Aegean variety generally called *mandilariá*, though possibly of a clone unto itself. The *rozé*, I gather, is relatively new to Kourounia, probably having been introduced after phylloxera. The *mávro*, on the other hand, is believed by the Kourouniotes to be virtually as old as their area, and it is difficult to dispute it. The grapes are dried in the sun for about a week before crushing, a method of concentrating sweetness that has been commonplace throughout the Aegean since early times:

But when Orion and Sirius are carried into mid-heaven, and rosy-fingered dawn sees Arcturus [September], then cut off all the grape-clusters, Perses, and bring them home. Show them to the sun ten days and ten nights: then cover them over for five, and on the sixth day draw off into vessels the gifts of joyful Dionysus.

(Hesiod, *Works and Days*, 7th century BC)

Some of the ancients thought Khios the first place where 'black' wine was made, which, even if unlikely, affirms a very long tradition of red wine. But no matter the pedigree of Kourounia's *mávro*, visiting wine lovers ought to be sure to remove their caps while there, for the lesson of the place is solemn: we never know when our own favourite wine, one we hope future generations will also know and appreciate, will be on the block, the victim of circumstances beyond its control.

South of Khios and just west of Samos, Ikaria rises out of the Aegean as a veritable block of granite, looking inhospitable and barely habitable. Yet inhabited it has been since before Homer. It is not an entirely stark place either, despite its wholly mountainous nature. Parts of the interior surprise with splurges of dark green woods, the landscape around Rakhes prompting the author Spiros Leotsakos, an Athenian admirer of Ikaria, to call it 'a piece of Switzerland in the middle of the Aegean'. Many visitors arrive for the island's curing, radium-charged thermal waters, rather than for the scenery, but there is also good reason for the enophile to begin his odyssey in the Aegean there, for Ikaria's claim to vinous fame is in its possession of what is not only one of the oldest known geographical designations in wine, but also the oldest in continuous use, Pramnian.

A settlement named Oinoi (Oenoe) prospered on Ikaria in ancient times, in the vicinity of today's community of Evdilos, near the north-central coast. Its earliest vineyards were south of there, close by what ancient writers mentioned as the *Prámni pétra* (Pramnos rock) which present-day villagers in the area point out as identical to the site they call *ta Bra*. The Pramnos name would seem to have been attached because of proximity to a more prominent topographical feature earlier named Pramnos. That name had a connection with the crest of mountains, gentle to the north, steep to the south, that runs parallel to Ikaria's southern coast. Now called Atheras, that mountainous span may have been known as Pramnos in ancient times. Or the name may have been applied to a peak or section about midway along Atheras; a local tradition claims that the mountain divide today called Prioni is the spot anciently identified as Pramnos. In any case, the Ikariotes, by a perfectly comprehensible logic, began exporting their surplus wine under the Pramnian name.

As Pramnian gained name recognition, other wine-producing areas of the Aegean also began using the Pramnos 'appellation' – it continued for so many hundreds of years that the misappropriation of certain wine place-names in modern times pales in comparison – with the eventual result that considerable confusion spread as to just what the name signified. By the time of Dioscorides, in the first century AD, the Pramnian name had become totally separated from the concept of geographic origin, for he associated it only with a generic kind of wine, the so-called *prótropon*, produced from the juice extracted by the weight of the grapes themselves, a type of wine which probably had no similarity to any grown on Ikaria. Athenaeus, in the third century AD, quoted the writer Eparhides, believed to have been an Ikariote of the early second century BC, rather as if to substantiate the Ikariote origin of the Pramnian name. Eparhides had described Pramnian as 'neither sweet nor fat, but dry, hard and of extraordinary strength', which recalls Aristophanes' earlier comment that Pramnian wines 'contract the eyebrows as well as the bowels'.

The Ikariotes apparently lost their stake in the Pramnian name at an early date. In the sixth century BC, Ikaria was plundered for its timber, another source of island wealth, by the autocrat Polycrates of Samos, to use for a fleet which he was having constructed. He also took the Ikariotes as slaves, especially to man his ships. It was the first in a long series of downturns in Ikaria's fortunes that had a bad effect on wine-growing. Already by the first century AD, Strabo found the island scarcely populated, and used mostly for cattle-grazing by the Samiotes. Over the centuries, the Ikariotes became homing seafarers for whom agriculture was a quite secondary activity. Although viticulture remained the island's main domestic activity until the end of the nineteenth century, it was sustained mostly by the market for Ikaria's black raisins. Around the turn of the century, nearly 900 hectares of vines were still producing, but the arrival of phylloxera in 1910 drastically reduced that area, and subsequent ideas of replanting have been perennially thwarted by incessant emigration. The island has under 100 hectares in vineyards now and, with some still producing grapes for raisins, Ikaria today has very little wine to its name, and no name in wine, not even within Greece.

The thought of Ikariote wine ever being bottled, let alone in the running for an appellation of origin, seems absolutely preposterous, notwithstanding its staggering credentials.

Vines on Ikaria are cultivated mostly on terraces flanking Atheras. The black varieties *koundoúra (mandilariá)* and *fokianí (fokianós)* – the latter also used for raisins – as well as the white *kolokitháto* and *rozakiá*, are grown. Today's *prámnio*, as some Ikariotes call it, is mostly dry red wine, and I suppose we are bound to wonder whether any of it could possibly bear any resemblance to ancient Pramnian. I cannot truly offer any advice on that, beyond referring to the ancient descriptions. I should mention the fact that the Ikariotes, by reason of their poverty and isolation, have retained some antique habits. Writing in 1678, Georgirenes mentioned that the Ikariotes were the only islanders of the Aegean who by that time were still unacquainted with barrels. Instead they stored their wine in earthen jars, which they routinely buried, completely covered, in the ground. At least one old man was doing just that a mere decade ago, to give the wine what to him remained a proper maturation. Furthermore, I am told by a recent Ikariote emigrant, totally unfamiliar with Athenaeus and Eparhides, of a special kind of aged red wine, produced in very minor quantity by just a few growers, that 'takes your head off after just a small glass of it'. Perhaps it is the buried kind. I can already see streams of wine buffs, spade in hand, setting off to dig up long jars in Ikariote fields!

CLASSICAL REFLECTIONS

Among the passages most likely to tickle the enophile perusing old books about the Aegean is one from Georgirenes concerning wine habits on hoary Ikaria. It might leave one wondering whether the Ikariotes could have been of the same stuff as ourselves:

> Their Wine is always made with a third part Water, and so very weak and small. When they drink it, so much as is thought sufficient is put into one large Bowl, and so passes round.
> (*A Description of the Present State of Samos, Nicaria, Patmos, and Mount Athos, 1678*)

Making a connection that might explain our interminable if urbane tableside disputes about 'best' wines, Leotsakos notes that even today the Ikariotes 'are neither friends of wine, nor of quarrelling'. The subject of the mingling of water and wine in any case makes one wonder about wine during antiquity.

The French viticulturalist Pierre Viala called Greece 'the country *par excellence* of sobriety'. Perhaps that is so, although Guérin earlier reported much backsliding on wine-deluged Samos in his day, but it must be supposed that a great deal of sobering experience accounts for it. How else, after all, could Aristotle have had sufficient opportunity to observe and conclude that wine lands the over-indulgent drinker face down, whereas barley beer causes him to pass out belly up? For that matter, it is most likely that Dionysus was converted in the first instance from a god of vegetative growth into the god of the vine and wine because the attribution to him of phenomena in plant life, particularly annual regeneration, or 'rebirth', made him seem responsible for the 'altered state' to which wine could transport man: *ékstasis* (rising out of one's ordinary state), *enthousiasmós* (achieving spiritual union with the gods), *manía* (yielding one's self-will to attractions emanating from outside one's self) all became integral to Dionysian worship. In order to tame wine, or rather to gain mastery over it, people learned to weaken its power by diluting it with water. Indeed, Athenaeus mentioned that people had had no appreciation of water before acquaintance with wine, whereas afterwards it was regarded as an ally of sorts. He went so far as to express his opinion that the watering of wine commercially, a practice already regarded as a ruse long before his time, may have originated not in profit-making, but out of 'forethought for the purchaser' (*The Deipnosophists*).

Although Aristotle noted that the particular pleasure of a wine's bouquet was spoiled through mixture with water (*Problems*), the two liquids were none the less regarded as compatible because they are not wholly alien to one another; the physician Galen observed that the capacity of two substances to mix and assimilate to one another was in fact a proof of their 'affinity' (*On the Natural Faculties*). Plato actually called wine a kind of water that had coursed through the plants of the earth (*Timaeus*), a notion which comported well with the sense of the ancient Greek term for wine, *ínos* (*oinos*), which was linked etymologically to a part of the vine, as befitted the early Greek wine drinkers' understanding of Dionysus's role. Athenaeus indicated that quite a few compositional overlaps were possible between waters and wines, as manifest mostly in similarities of feel, but sometimes also in physiological effect, with an occasional water even sparking a giddiness he likened to intoxication. The ancients therefore spoke of some waters as being *inódis* (*oinodes*), that is, winy or vinous. By the same token, some wines participated more than others in the nature of water (*ýdor*) and could on that account be mentioned as *ydatódis*, or watery.

The goal in mixing must generally have been as stated by Aristotle, who wrote that 'well-mixed wine obscures all perception of water, and only gives a sensation of soft wine' (*Problems*). Consequently, practices pertaining to the mixture of water and wine usually varied according to the specific water and wine at hand. For example, Hippocrates, in speaking of the virtues of 'light' waters of altitudinous places, noted that 'the wine they can stand is but little' (*Ancient Medicine*). Sometimes, however, circumstantial factors may also have influenced mixing, perchance even more in favour of the water than the wine:

> Five, indeed, is in the ratio 3:2, three parts of water being mixed with two parts of wine: three is in the ratio 2:1, two parts of water being mixed with one of wine; and four – three parts of water being poured into one of wine – this is a ratio of 4:3, a drink for some group of sensible magistrates in the prytaneion, or logicians, their brows contracted as they meditate upon syllogistic conversion, a sober and feeble mixture.
>
> (Aristion, in Plutarch's *Moralia*: 'Table-talk'; 'No one attacked
> Aristion's remarks for clearly his talk was play.')

No unmixed wine was poured at symposia in particular, yet even in more ordinary circumstances mixture was so much the general rule that the drinking of unmixed wine, *ákratos*, became conspicuous, and thereby lent its name to the morning meal, *akrátisma*, at which its use remained common, if mostly as a liquid medium in which to take solid foods, or else just to moisten them. Mixed wine, *kekraménos ínos* (*oinos*), was prepared in the vessel called *krátir* (mixing bowl), a procedure called *krásis* (mixing). It was from this terminology that wine acquired a colloquial name that has come down to the modern Greeks as *krasí*, and has supplanted *ínos* (*oinos*) in ordinary speech.

GASTRONOMIC NOTES

I do not believe it should detract from the epicurean allure of the Eastern Sporades to observe that they do not rank in culinary stature as they did when Ionia was at its acme and Khios, reportedly the first Greek place to use purchased slaves, had freed itself from drudgery and earned a mention by Timocles as being 'by far the best in inventing dainty dishes' (Athenaeus, *The Deipnosophists*). I remember with special pleasure enjoying on Samos, at an apparently unnamed *tavérna* to which I was taken, situated up a flight of stairs in Paleokastro, what was quite simply the best seafood meal I have ever had, in spite of the resinated Samian muscat poured to accompany it.

> My poor Lucius used to amuse himself by concocting delicacies for me; his pheasant pasties with their skilful blending of ham and spice bore witness to an art which is as exacting as that of a musician or painter, but I could not help regretting the unadulterated flesh of the fine bird. Greece knew better about such things: her resin-steeped wine, her bread sprinkled with sesame seed, fish grilled at the very edge of the sea and unevenly blackened by the fire, or seasoned here and there by the grit of sand, all satisfied the appetite alone without surrounding by too many complications this simplest of our joys. In the merest hole of a place in Aegina or Phaleron I have tasted food so fresh that it remained divinely clean despite the dirty fingers of the tavern waiter.
>
> (Marguerite Yourcenar, *Memoirs of Hadrian*)

I concede, though, that one is usually better off being invited into a native's home, even a wine-grower's humble abode, than having to be confined to a *tavérna* perspective.

The high point of Eastern Sporadic cuisine today is probably the mushrooms that spring up plentifully in the dense forests of Samos and Ikaria. Numerous sorts of mushrooms, called *manitária* generally in Greek, are to be found there, and each edible variety, graced with its own name, is prepared in a way, or ways, deemed particularly suitable to it. The subject so absorbed one official of the Agricultural Bank of Greece on Samos whom I met, that he had developed an amateur ethnographical interest in it. Once, as we sat in the café of the high-altitude first-rank muscat village of Manolates, drawing the puzzled attention of the regulars, he played me what seemed an endless tape-recording of Samiote villagers describing their myriad habits of collecting and preparing mushrooms. It was too much for me to digest in a single sitting, and I am consequently scarcely less ignorant on the subject now than I was then. Unfortunately, in looking over the standard *tavérna* menu, one might never guess that Samos and Ikaria are the centre of Greek mycology.

The list of special foodstuffs from the Eastern Sporades includes several kinds of table olives and cheese. Khios has a most distinctive sort of olive, as peculiar in appearance as it is in taste. Of a nutty flavour, with a more or less gritty texture, these olives appear wrinkled and brown, hence their name *khourmádes* (dates). Traditionally, they are collected following hard rains and high winds that knock them off the trees. Samos offers a rather round, brownish-green olive that is well regarded in Greece. Cheeses are headed by *Khiakí kopanistí* (Khian pounded), a somewhat malleable, though not quite soft, sheep's-milk cheese, made by kneading every few days over a two- to three-month period until a fungus forms, giving it an idiosyncratic flavour akin to that of very ripe blue cheeses: in fact it is sometimes referred to as Khian Roquefort. However, as there is very little of the genuine article, ersatz versions, usually called just *kopanistí*, are more commonly sold in Greece. They may or may not be entirely of sheep's milk, and they owe their sharpness to the addition of capsicum, rather than to the original *kopanistí* technique. On Samos, goat cheeses are particularly good. Natives sometimes eat them while sipping sweet muscat of Glyko or Imiglyko type; the taste contrast parallels that of *prosciutto* with melon. Mytilini, whose olive oil is touted as the best of the Eastern Sporades, is a major producer and exporter of *ladotýri* (oil-cheese), a hard sheep's-milk cheese that acquires a special flavour and texture by curing in olive oil.

Two distilled drinks from the eastern islands have a considerable reputation in Greece. One is Mytilini's *oúzo*, the aniseed-flavoured spirit now associated with Greece nearly worldwide. A very great deal of *oúzo* is produced and bottled by the Distillers' Union of Mytilene (*sic*), or EPOM, which also exports abroad. On Mytilini, the excellent local sardines (*sardélles*) are highly thought of as a *mezé*, or tidbit, to accompany the *oúzo*. The other drink comes from Khios and is a close relative of *oúzo*. It is *mastíkha*, which is flavoured with mastic in addition to aniseed. The world's mastic production is wholly concentrated in the southernmost part of the island, in the *mastikokhóra*, or mastic country. The bushy little trees, which require considerable expert care, yield their valuable sap drop by drop on to the ground, where it hardens, to be collected later for cleaning and eventual dispatch to world markets for chewing-gum. For reasons I have never quite been able to fathom, unless it is that in the days before toothpaste mastic was appreciated as a breath-freshener in Ottoman harems, *mastíkha* is considered rather a lady's drink, or at any rate something of a feminine version of *oúzo*. I am reminded of Aristotle's comment on the difference between wine and barley beer. Anyway, mastic may also be taken as a 'spoon sweet' (*glykó tou koutalioú*), in which case it is referred to as *ypovrýkhio* (submarine), because instead of sipping the water that is always served with spoon sweets, the habit in this case alone is to dip a spoonful into the glass.

2

Rhodes and the Dodecanese

In the greater part of [Rhodes] the coast inclines imperceptibly. . . . Most of the slopes are covered with thorny bushes or bramble. Some of them afford vineyards which still produce the perfumed wine sought by the ancients. It is of a very pleasant taste and leaves an exquisite flavour [bouquet] in the mouth . . . It would be easy to multiply [the vineyards], and cover with them hills of a great extent, which are lying without cultivation.
(Claude Savary, French traveller, Letters on Greece, 1788)

RHODES (RODOS)

South of Samos and Ikaria the Aegean grows thicker with islands. Beginning at Patmos an almost linearly arranged string of them appears on the horizon at regular intervals. Collectively called the Dodecanese, or the 'Twelve Isles', the group curves slightly to the south-east, as though following the south-western coast of Asia Minor. Nowadays they seem a very remote and minor outpost of the Greek state, but during antiquity their position so close to the Asian mainland enabled certain of the Dodecanese to gain a significance in the Greek world out of all proportion to their size. The natural centre of the group is Rhodes, which is quite the largest member, and just about the easternmost of them. By reason of its forward position to the south-east, Rhodes was a major contact point between the Greeks and other civilizations to the east, and earlier had actually been settled by the Phoenicians. The island might therefore have been among the earliest spots in the Aegean to receive the vine and vinify its fruit, and was a major trader in wine by the seventh century BC. Its maritime prowess, which perhaps was acquired in no little part through its wine trade, later encouraged Rhodes to undertake a

40

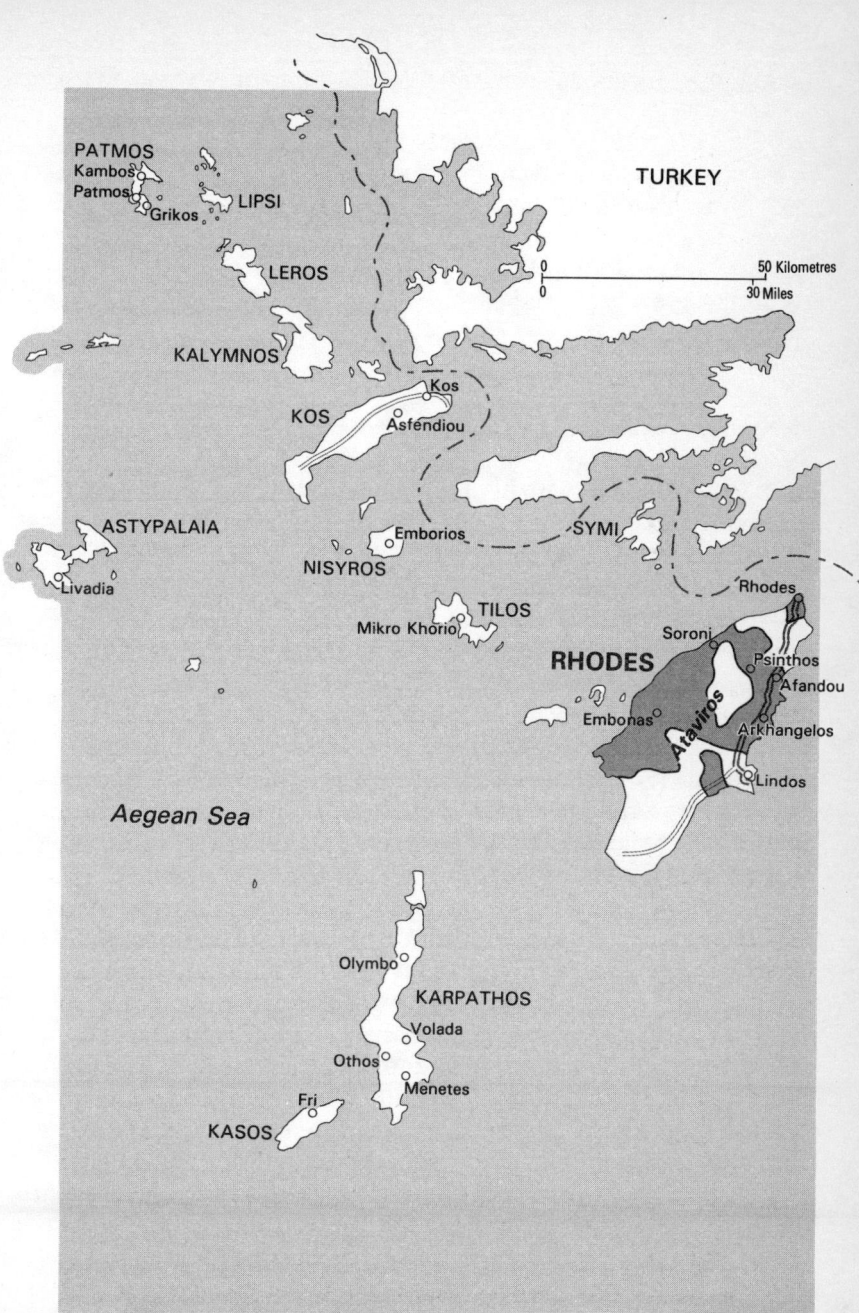

The Dodecanese

voluminous transit trade in grain, which brought it unparalleled wealth. It was around that time, in the third century BC, that the short-lived Colossus of Rhodes spanned the harbour entrance. Rhodes's own products were apparently pulled along by the impetus of its transit trade, and reached as many and as distant places as did its grain transhipments. Foremost among the native goods traded was wine, carried off in amphoras marked specifically as Rhodian, fragments of which have been unearthed virtually throughout the ancient world.

Later wine-growers of Rhodes also prospered. While under the administration of the crusading Knights of St John, who established themselves on the island in 1309 to avail themselves of its strategic location, the local farmers benefited from the opportunity of provisioning the chevaliers with both food and drink. It was in that period too that Rhodes began participating in the lucrative malmsey trade. As late as the mid-eighteenth century the visiting Lord Charlemont found what seemed to him 'a very great quantity of excellent wine'. However, by that time Rhodes was firmly under Ottoman control, and it was only the attraction of revenues from the malmsey trade that kept the local rulers from choking off wine production. Rhodian farmers, including producers of table wines, generally faced only disincentives under the Ottomans, because when the Knights of St John surrendered the island in 1522, after resisting the Ottoman siege for 177 days, the new rulers punished Rhodes by granting it none of the privileges enjoyed by others of the Dodecanese that had acquiesced in Ottoman rule.

Just a few decades after Lord Charlemont's visit, Savary found Rhodian agriculture in distress ('And with the destruction of agriculture goes also the destruction of all arts and crafts which she initiates and for which she supplies the basis and the material' : Plutarch, *Moralia*, 'Dinner of the Seven Wise Men'). The ruling pasha of the day would do nothing to stimulate farming, for reasons which were transparent. Enjoying a monopoly on trade, the pasha was more than satisfied to keep output low and prices high, and had no desire to invest revenues rather than consume them, knowing that only his successor – who, under the Ottoman system, would not be a hereditary one – would reap the rewards of enhancing the island's agricultural potential. Subsequent rulers, ever more independent of the Porte, and proportionately less concerned about the future of the land in their charge, only exacerbated the situation Savary had found.

Thus, by the middle of the nineteenth century Rhodian wine-growing reached its nadir:

> well made . . . the red wines of Rhodes would be excellent *vins de table* which would not lack having an outlet in Europe; but this culture is little diffused and in most of the villages is even unknown.
> (Guérin, *Étude sur l'île de Rhodes*, 1856)

The occasion of deliverance for the Dodecanese was the Italo-Turkish War of 1912. As a result of its victory, Italy acquired the group. Italian rule was not without its failings. Animosity was stirred by efforts at administrative Italianization, including the undoing of local landholding customs, which the Ottomans had left intact. Many inhabitants of the Dodecanese departed in frustration and protest. None the less, the Italians were aware of the squandering of economic resources under the Ottomans, and took a special interest in upgrading agriculture, especially on the main island of Rhodes, where an Italian agricultural colony was established, rather in the nature of a model farming community. Improvement of vineyard cultivation and wine-making figured prominently in Italian visions of the development of Rhodes, and the task was eased by the circumstance that Rhodes had been, and still is, spared phylloxera.

A most significant development for Rhodian wine occurred in 1928, when a private society called CAIR, the Agricultural and Industrial Company of Rhodes, was formed by a group of foreign entrepreneurs for the purpose of processing agricultural goods, including wine. Although the Dodecanese passed out of Italian control in 1943, to be incorporated by Greece in 1947, CAIR lives on as the wine-production arm of the Union of Agricultural Cooperatives of the Dodecanese. Headquartered in the town of Rhodes, CAIR buys over 90 per cent of all grapes marketed on the island, and turns out about 90,000 hectolitres of wine annually. Thanks to its vigorous marketing programme throughout Greece, and on export markets as well, CAIR has kept viticulture profitable for Rhodite growers. Indeed Rhodes was among the few areas of Greece that experienced an extension of vineyard land in the post-Second World War years. CAIR may also be largely credited with having put Rhodes in a position to gain appellation of origin rights, which it did in 1971, for qualifying dry white, dry red, and sweet muscat wines.

More fundamental than CAIR to recent Rhodian success in wine is the same factor that worked to the island's advantage in antiquity: its natural environment. Rhodes is singularly blessed for viticulture. It has the longest season of summery weather in Greece – which keeps the droves of tourists coming – and enjoys a particularly high level of insolation. More sunny days and fewer rainy ones occur there than anywhere else in the Aegean, and threats to grape quality are parried by exposition, air currents, and moisture. The most esteemed fruit for quality dry wine is grown mostly on north-facing sites along the north-western side of the Mount Ataviros range that bisects the island from north-east to south-west, which to a large extent forestalls the potentially harmful effects of the insolation on sugar-acid balance in the grapes. The considerable threat of excessive soil temperature in particular is allayed by sea breezes that cool the land twice a day during the May to September ripening period. Also, owing to the influence of the highlands of Asia Minor, a concentrated period of rainfall occurs in between tourist seasons, such that more rain falls on Rhodes annually than in most of the southern Aegean. The island gets twice as much rain as Attica, and it takes a long while to trickle down through Ataviros.

Varietal make-up goes a long way towards bringing to fruition the potential for grape quality offered by the environment of Rhodes. The island is among the most varietally uniform of the archipelago, which is especially remarkable if its size is considered. The two main grape varieties are the white *athíri* and the red *mandilariá*, which together account for over 90 per cent of the approximately 2,000 hectares of vineyards. Both varieties are found widely in the southern Aegean, but rarely adapted so well as to be able to yield dry varietal wines of quality, and nowhere on the scale of Rhodes. Rhodes is in fact likely to remain the only place that produces any varietal *athíri* wine, and also the only one to be granted appellation rights for dry varietal *mandilariá* wine. At present, nearly 1,100 hectares of *athíri* and 600 hectares of *mandilariá* are cultivated in their respective appellative zones, which overlap considerably, at least as regards the villages included in them. In elevation, the vineyards whose fruit qualifies for appellation white or red dry wines differ markedly, the *athíri* occupying the high ground, and the *mandilariá* the lower.

The *athíri* is of particular interest for its apparent antiquity; indeed it may have begun its accommodation to Rhodian conditions a very long time ago, very likely with the variety which the ancients knew as *thiriakí*, so called after the island of Thira, or Santorini; it has been supposed that the name would have evolved as *thíraia* . . . *thíri* . . . *athíri*. The *thiriakí* seems to have been generally associated with sweet wine in ancient times, and indeed this is the sort of wine for which the *athíri* has mostly been used in the southern Aegean in the modern era. On Rhodes, the variety succeeds best in the range of 300–800 metres above sea level in the north-western area, where ample acidity is assured in the resultant wines. CAIR produces annually nearly 30,000 hectolitres of 12° dry *athíri* wine that qualifies for the Rhodes appellation, using grapes from the villages of Embonas, Ayios Isidoros, Kritinia, Siana, Monolithos and Apollona, all of which are places specified by the appellative regulation. Of them, Embonas has the best reputation for white wine.

CAIR uses contemporary technology in making its white appellation wine, which it bottles under the Ilios label. (Ilios was formerly called Lindos, a name still encountered in some wine and travel books. The earlier name was changed because it gave a false impression of the area of the island from which the wine hails.) In a healthy state, Ilios is of a lustrous, pale straw colour, and should appear substantially so through the clear glass bottle. In my experience, the vintage-dated Ilios offers little reward for being kept, not even when laid down, much less when standing upright several years as it might in a Greek neighbourhood grocery, but the maxim 'age before beauty' is refuted by Ilios's scent. I might call it a mild blend of herby and floral smells, but they defy individual analysis, instead comprising a whole that might truly be identified only as what it is . . . *athíri* of Rhodes. 'Sweating glass' serving temperatures intended to simulate crispness through coolness neutralize the light but clear aroma of Ilios, and more generally upset a balance of flavour features pertaining to impressions of both delicacy and strength.

Its various characteristics recommend Ilios as an aperitif wine, especially when appetizers to be served are substantial, though bitterish or aromatically pungent ones can distract. The *khourmádes* olives of Khios might be appropriate, and, among cheeses, the cow's-milk types, especially milder ones, including Syrian/Armenian 'string' cheese. Grilled mushroom caps stuffed with savoury fillings can also win friends for Ilios. It is also a good accompaniment for main courses, and I might suggest the Greek version of stuffed cabbage (*lakhanodolmádes*) with minced lamb in the filling and *avgolémono* (egg-lemon) sauce. Meatless stuffed tomatoes and peppers (*domátes/piperiés yemistés*) might also be considered, which always ought to be served tepid. Generally, parsley, dill, thyme and rosemary are seasonings to look to for aromatic congruence with Ilios, especially with fish.

Like the *athíri*, the red *mandilariá*, the second major grape variety of Rhodes, may have arrived from the Cyclades. It is generally called *amoryianó* on Rhodes, suggesting that it came by way of Amorgos, to the north-west. In any case the *mandilariá* could be said to have had an even happier adaptation on Rhodes than the *athíri*, in that its success in giving dry red wines all on its own is very sporadic. On Rhodes, however, the late-ripening *mandilariá* is able to ripen fully at the relatively lower altitudes, so that dry wines produced from it there do not necessarily lack in alcoholic degree, which is often a problem with dry *mandilariá* wines grown elsewhere. The vineyards for *mandilariá* are mostly situated between 50 and 300 metres above sea level, and owing to the northern exposure and breezes, Rhodian reds can have quite sufficiently lively acidity as well. With those considerations in mind, the villages of Fanes, Soroni, Kalavarda, Damatria, Tholos, Embonas, Kritinia, Siana, Monolithos, Apollona, Ayios Isidoros, Maritsa and Salakos are included in the appellation zone for Rhodian red wine. Soroni and Embonas are generally regarded as the best of them. CAIR uses *mandilariá* grapes primarily from the first five mentioned villages to produce its appellation red wine, an 11.7° alcohol wine fermented on skins only, and bottled after one year in oak, which is the minimum maturation requirement specified in the appellative rules. It is marketed under the Chevalier de Rhodes label, with vintage date. Nearly 20,000 hectolitres are produced annually.

Even before the advent of the modern cellar on Rhodes, the island had a good reputation for its red wine. The English traveller William Turner, writing in 1820, 'thought it very good; it is a sharp-tasted red wine, with a little sweetness'. The sweetness, it would seem, is a feature of the past now, assuming that Turner meant it literally. Dry red wine is all one finds today, and that is very true of Chevalier de Rhodes. Unusual among southern Aegean reds for its scant fleshiness of texture, Chevalier manages all the same to register vividly on the mouth surfaces, in its way recalling Turner's phrase, 'sharp-tasted'. Especially when young, the always orange-seeking, garnet Chevalier spreads its sensations across the entire upper surface of the tongue. Given three to six years of bottle age – how unfortunate that it is rarely given the chance – Chevalier mellows to achieve a balance with aromatic flavour. At the same time, the earlier 'sweet-spicy' bouquet gives way, to a greater or lesser extent, to a fragrance sometimes reminiscent of tulips, but usually at least floral in a general way, no matter what the vintage or bottle. The result is a wine with a most unusual and harmonious juxtaposition of a delicate freshness of aromatic flavour and stalwart tactile sensations. I would not care, though, to challenge the verdict of a Gallic gastronomic duo who assess Chevalier – on the basis of how many vintages, I do not know – as being on a par with a *petit* St-Émilion. Certainly anyone who can sit on Rhodes and think of St-Émilion while looking at, sniffing or tasting Chevalier has a very great tolerance for sun, and should be given due respect and credence.

The turnabout in the character of Chevalier de Rhodes as it ages is notable among Greek reds worthy of cellaring, so much so that it is all too easy for an attendant of it to become peevishly finicky about the bottle's age when it comes to putting together a meal. I have succumbed my share of times, and would recommend a young Chevalier for certain spreadables, like some of the commonly available herbed cheeses – but do not neglect *tapenade*, the Mediterranean crushed-olive spread. For the older wine, have a mild cheese like havarti with dill. Greek beef specialities flavoured with cinnamon or cloves, like *stifádo*, seem ideal for a young bottle, while pot roasts of many descriptions will do as well with the older wine. Young meats such as veal are appropriate for an older Chevalier, and can be flavoured somewhat robustly, as in paprika schnitzel. Chevalier always seems to please with lamb, but forethought moves me to prefer an older bottle with barbecued marinated lamb. As for vegetables, try somewhat abrasive and bitterish ones, such as spinach or zucchini with the skin on, perhaps flavoured with a little tomato sauce and nutmeg: I have fond memories of an earlyish Chevalier drunk with artichokes in a dilute, well-herbed tomato sauce.

Among its top-of-the-range wines, CAIR saves its very best for last in the course of a meal, offering its muscat wine as a finish. It would be placed, no doubt, far higher *vis-à-vis* others in its category than would either Chevalier de Rhodes or Ilios. Given the warm climate of Rhodes, sweet wine has been produced there since antiquity, and the *moskháto áspro* of Greece and the *trani* muscat introduced by the Italians are cultivated for sweet wine today. Both muscat varieties must be used for the wine to qualify for a Rhodian muscat appellation of origin. Within the appellation zone, they are grown on fewer than

10 hectares at present, all lying between 50 and 100 metres above sea level. The villages within the zone are situated both on the east-central coast and in the west: going anti-clockwise from the north-west, they are Fanes, Apollona, Embonas, Monolithos, Lardos, Arkhangelos, Afandou and Psinthos. The latter place is especially intriguing from the point of view of whether the ancient *psíthios* wine might have been a muscat [see p. 19], since Psinthos, which is presumed to be named for the profusion of *apsínthion* (wormwood) found there, could have lent its name to the vine of that name. Alas, even if it had, that would not prove that *psíthios* was a muscat.

CAIR produces about 500 hectolitres of appellation Rhodes muscat annually, and markets it under the Muscat de Rhodes label. The grapes come from around the villages of Arkhangelos and Lardos on the east-central coast, the sunnier side of the island where the breezes are that much more crucial to quality, and Fanes on the north-western coast. The wine is of an orange-gold colour, with an aroma of floral and sweet-spicy smells, the typical coriander tendency of muscat seeming to me to be quite distinct in it, though not in isolation. It is similar to Samos Glyko in sweetness and texture, but usually firmer and possessed of somewhat more vinous force. It has a place beside the popular Greek *glyká tou tapsioú* (pan sweets, that is, oriental pastries), but I think it at least as good with carrot cake. At any event, one should not miss Muscat de Rhodes while on the island. Drinking it, one can understand just what Savary was talking about 200 years ago.

CAIR also produces lesser-quality red and white appellation wines, on the Rodos label. A rosé (*mandilariá*) called Moulin has also appeared and, inevitably, a Retsina, from *athíri*, although the Rhodians traditionally do not resinate their wines. Additionally, there is a fortified wine called Amandia, which is meant to resemble a wine of port type. It is made from *mandilariá* (60 per cent) and the red *diminítis* (40 per cent), the latter variety probably being a local variant of the *liátiko* of eastern Crete, which has a long history of use for sweet wines. CAIR takes a special pride in its *brut* and *demi-sec* sparkling *athíri* wines under the CAIR label, which are the only sparkling wines of Greece made by the *méthode champenoise*, and more than decently underscore both CAIR's technical capability and its skill in using the environment of Rhodes to advantage.

Besides CAIR, the small private firm of Emery, belonging to the Triantafyllos family, has operated a winery at Embonas since 1968.

Emery has no vineyards of its own and buys all its grapes in Embonas. The firm makes both red and white appellation wines, and has two labels in both cases. The higher-quality and higher-alcohol wines are the 12° red Lacosta and white Grand Maître de Rhodes, of which about 2,000 and 10,000 hectolitres respectively are produced each year. They are vintage-dated. A lesser red and white, both at 11°, are released under the Rodos label. Additionally, a reserve red wine of 12.5° is produced in a quantity of about 900 hectolitres annually, and aged for three years, including one to one and a half in barrel. It is marketed under the Kava Emery label. There is also a *brut* sparkling wine under the Emery label.

THE DODECANESE

Apart from Rhodes, the islands of the south-eastern Aegean are mostly very small and unproductive, the exception being sizeable and very fertile Kos, the garden of the Aegean, and the original home of Cos or romaine lettuce. During antiquity, the island had a considerable reputation for wine, both red and white, apparently dry in the former case and sweet in the latter, but in that era its economy was thriving and its population numbered over 150,000. Hardly more than 20,000 people inhabit Kos now, and a semblance of prosperity has only recently returned after a dismal period of several hundred years. Kos evidently suffered a great deal during Ottoman times, to such an extent that in the early nineteenth century Turner, who found only white wine when visiting Kos, mentioned it as being 'in the most wretched condition of any of the Greek islands I have seen'. The relative fecundity of Kos drew to it many Turkish inhabitants, who comprised fully five-eighths of the population when Turner was there, and stayed on well beyond his day. Kos was still about half-Turkish until nearly midway through the twentieth century. The Moslem presence, which extended into the countryside, had a negative impact on viticulture on the island as a whole, and Kos was also visited by phylloxera. But a good initial recovery from its recent past has been made, and Kos is now producing bottled wines in an amount of about 5,000 hectolitres annually, all by the Vinicultural Cooperative of Kos (Vinko).

The winery of the Cooperative is located near the north-eastern coast by Kos town, but all the grapes it vinifies are produced at

Asfendiou, located in the east-central part of the interior of the island. The vineyards thereabouts are on the northern foothills of Mount Dikaios, and lie mostly between 100 and 300 metres above sea level, on a shallow layer of silty clay. The varieties grown are the wine grapes *mandilariá*, which is called *amouryianó* on Kos, and *athíri*, and the dessert grapes *rozakí áspro* and *soultanína*, all of which are used for the Cooperative's wines: Apellis, a dry red made from *mandilariá*; Glafkos, a dry white from *athíri, rozakí*, and *soultanína*; Retsina, made from a similar mixture, and comprising half of the output; and Vereniki, a semi-sweet, fortified red made from the three white varieties in addition to *mandilariá*. Apellis, produced in a quantity of about 1,200 hectolitres annually, is a 12.5° red that is usually aged in barrel for two years before bottling, although it is not bottled with a vintage date. It presents a smooth bouquet, if one less amenable to bottle age than its counterpart *mandilariá* wines from Rhodes. Could the Cooperative lure the villagers of Asfendiou away from the attraction of tourist-catering and increase plantings of *mandilariá* in the most suitable area, Apellis might perhaps be worked up into a wine that would draw attention to Kos once more.

Neither in ancient times nor in recent centuries were the other islands of the Dodecanese significant traders in wine, if they ever had much to export at all. Furthermore, most were visited by phylloxera, and emigration has been scarcely less crushing. Only very small areas of vines remain: on Patmos, in the north at Kambos, and in the southeast at Grikos and Diakofti; at Katsadia on the south-eastern coast of Lipsi; in the upland village of Emborios on Nisyros; by Livadia on the south-eastern part of the western sac of Astypalaia; around Mikro Khorio on Tilos; and to the south-west of Fri on Kasos. The varieties grown throughout the islands are primarily the *mandilariá* and *fokianó* for reddish wines, and the *athíri* and *rozakí* for whites. Retsina has been making inroads in the Dodecanese in recent years, notably on Symi. At the end of the eighteenth century, Savary called the island's wine 'good' and made no mention of resination, which would have been an exotic feature of the sort he was inclined to note, but Symi for the most part makes retsina these days. However, the Symiotes have special praise for unresinated wines grown on their satellite island of Teftlousa, to the south, which belongs to the Monastery of Panormitis on the Symiote coast opposite. It would seem a good reason to pay the monks a visit.

Among the lesser wine producers of the Dodecanese, one especially worth a wine buff's exploration is Karpathos, to the south-west of Rhodes. It was spared phylloxera, and its grape varieties predictably represent a transition between Rhodes and Crete: the red *mandilariá* and *fokianó*, and the white *athíri, thrápsa* (the *thrapsathíri* of eastern Crete), *kolokitháta, rozakí,* and *moskháto áspro.* Sweetish wines of the mountain villages of Volada, Othos, and Menetes should be sought. Although neither resinated, nor piny in flavour, they are produced with pieces of pine bark added to the must during fermentation in clay jars. For the thoroughly modern enophile engulfed by the technological hubris of the late twentieth century they can be absolutely devastating in the deliciousness they sometimes show.

CLASSICAL REFLECTIONS

In choosing Ilios, sun, as the name of a wine, CAIR of Rhodes has evoked the island's one-time association with the Sun-god, much as was done anciently by Rhodian wine traders, who used a depiction of the sun as an emblem to identify their amphorae. But the name also seems to be something of a cultural Freudian slip, in that it reveals a Greek slant on wine that is bound up in the eternal Aegean scene. It is a perspective older than the ancients' notion of an alliance of sun, fire and wine, yet fresher than the words of a recent Greek popular song, 'I want you to be an eagle, that the light of the sun be your wine.'

One kind of light has never gone out in the Greek space: that diaphanous Aegean sunlight.

> The mountains, the valley, the sea play a secondary role. The light is the resplendent Sober Dionysus who is dismembered and suffers, then rejoins his parts and triumphs. The entire scene of Greece seems to have come to be just that he might perform.
>
> (Nikos Kazantzakis, *Journey to the Morea*)

That performance caused the ancients to be fascinated by vision in a way that may seem strange to us because of the immediacy and intensity of their experience of it:

> In all probability the most active stream of [bodily] emanations [that produce sensation] is that which passes out through the eye. For vision, being of an enormous swiftness and carried by an

essence that gives off a flame-like brilliance, diffuses a wondrous influence. In consequence, man both experiences and produces many effects through his eyes. He is possessed and governed by either pleasure or displeasure exactly in proportion to what he sees.

(Plutarch, *Moralia*, 'Table-talk')

Thus did sight go to the heart of wine appreciation, and perhaps influence wine-growing itself.

The ancients saw that light, or rather its source, the sun, was of crucial significance to wine. Sunlight imparted to wine a fire to which was attributed both appearance and physiological effects. The Sun-god's 'tears amber-beaming' become 'the Wine-god's fire', and then 'the wine's flame', to borrow Euripides' metaphors. Wine's intimate, direct link with the sun's fire caused brilliance to become associated with wine as an essential quality, much in the sense meant by Sappho when she said that 'brightness and honour [the "natural properties of virtue"] belong to my yearning for the sun' (Athenaeus, *The Deipnosophists*). By way of alluding to its sparkling aspect, wine gained the description *éthopa* (*aithopa*), since, as Euripides related, one of the Sun-god's horses was called Aithopa (Fiery). It may have been to bring the vine closer to the sun, thereby shortening Aithopa's haul, that early Aegean vine-tenders originally moved its cultivation up mountainsides.

Colour, which Plato (*Timaeus*) defined as 'a flame which streams off from every sort of body', was also cause for wonderment under Aegean skies. Athenaeus distinguished four cardinal wine colours: *lefkós* (white), *kirrós* (tawny), *erythrós* (red) and *melénas* (black). He mostly referred to Clearclus to explain these colours. The commonality of the two extremes was the absence of reddishness, Clearclus having remarked that both water and milk are called *lefkós*, while identifying *melénas*, which literally means 'inky', with mulberry juice. In between those two was a range of more ambiguous hues in which orange or red was apparent, *kirrós* by its very name indicating the brownish yellow of bee's wax, while *erythrós* described red proper ('the radiance of [a certain sort of] fire through the moisture with which it is mingled gives blood-colour, which we call "red" ' – Plato, (*Timaeus*). To *erythrós* belonged the distinction of being specifically identified with wine, Clearclus having used wine as his example of that colour, the way he did other potable liquids for *lefkós* and *melénas*. But in wine of any colour the ancients would have expected chromatic nuances that amounted to visual analogues, and foretellers, of a *goût de terroir* ('taste of the locale'), much as when Theophrastus (*Enquiry into Plants*) observed that the colour as well as the scent of flowers varies with locality. It is what comes of a melding of grape varieties with environments, but a melding judged and directed by people who look at wine in the light of their place.

GASTRONOMIC NOTES

Surely Rhodes's gardens, which are second only to those of Kos in Dodecanese lore, must be mentioned as a primary source of raw material for the native kitchen. And it ought to be noted as well that Rhodian olive oil is generally thought the best of the Dodecanese. As concerns cooking as such, however, I would be remiss not to take into account Rhodes's special history, which brought to it long-lingering people from both west and east: Franks, Sephardic Jews, Turks, Armenians, Italians. A richly cosmopolitan streak consequently winds its way through Rhodian cuisine, although usually in subtle ways, since the foreigners' proclivities have largely been adapted to the local environment and customs, rather than preserved in isolation in alien dishes.

While not generally sharing in Rhodes's reputation for culinary skill, most of the smaller of the Dodecanese are known for certain specialities. Several islands are appreciated by Greek seafood lovers: Kos, Astypalaia, Leros, Kasos and Kastelorizo. By reason of gastronomic history, first mention in that category should perhaps go to Kasos, since fishermen there still pull in the *skáros*, which was the alpha and omega of fish as far as the classical gourmet was concerned. But Kastelorizo has staunch fans of its oysters (*strídia*) and other bivalves. Astypalaia and Leros are also known for small game: hare, partridge, doves. Spit-roasted wild goat of Teftlousa is prized on Symi. At Easter, the villagers on Nisyros prepare a local version of *kapamás*, which consists of goat meat baked in a deep, open clay pot. Generally in the Dodecanese, and on most other southern Aegean islands as well, Easter lamb is also baked in the traditional ovens, rather than spit-roasted as on the mainland. But on 1 May (*Protomayiá*), the Nisyriotes celebrate by roasting a suckling pig on the spit (*vrouláki tis soúvlas*). Several of the Dodecanese, especially Kalymnos, Kasos and Symi, are known for their honey – Kalymnos at least since Strabo's time. A confection made with honey and sesame, *sisamómeli*, is typical of several of the lesser Dodecanese, but that of Kasos is particularly well thought of. On Karpathos, *sisamómeli* is embellished with a filling of sugar-coated chickpeas.

As demonstrated by its wine-making, Karpathos has preserved some very archaic habits, and that holds true in the kitchen as well. The best-known Karpathian speciality is *psilokoúlouro*, which is a ring (*kouloúra*) of sesame-studded, rather thin (*psilós*), braided strips of dough baked in the characteristic island ovens. *Psilokoúlouro* is appreciated for its peculiarly chewy texture, and is reported to have great keeping powers, a veritable *pain de garde*. The most traditional of all Karpathian villages is Olymbo, high up in the north. It is there that a visitor is most likely to come upon the dish called *khóndros*, whose mere mention might stir readers of Athenaeus who recall his numerous references to 'gruel', which was called *khóndros*. The Karpathian dish of that name consists of meat cooked with milled wheat, and one must conclude that it was food like this that nurtured Homeric heroes. Weddings at Olymbo are celebrated by roasting oxen over charcoal, which has become a rare practice in Greece in modern times since their scarcity has made oxen too valuable as draught animals to slaughter just for the table. The custom at Olymbo could be a relic of ancient tradition, perhaps even linked to the slaughter of oxen that was part of some early rituals honouring 'ox-horn Dionysus' and 'bull-shaped Dionysus' (Nonnos, *Dionysiaca*). The connection of Dionysus with oxen may have arisen from his identification in mytholgy as the pioneer of plowing and sowing (Plutarch, *Moralia*, 'The Roman Questions'), which had probably grown out of his earlier role as the god of vegetative growth. But I suppose the Olymbians are not too concerned with all that when they sit down to a wedding feast.

3
Crete

The wines of Candia are excellent, reds, whites, and clarets . . . the wines of this clime have quite enough tartness to offset their lusciousness; this lusciousness, far from being flat, is accompanied by a delicious balm that makes those who have really tasted through the wines of Candia scorn all other wine.
  (Joseph Tournefort, French traveller, *Relation d'un Voyage du Levant*, 1717)

The bounds of the Aegean world have ever been fixed to the south by the island of Crete, long known in the West by its Venetian name, Candia. Although an integral member of the Archipelago, and one that typifies it in many ways, Crete can hardly be considered just another Aegean island. It lies off from the rest, actually in a sea named after it, the Sea of Crete, which rivals the Aegean proper in extent. It is by far the largest island as well, and because most of its terrain other than the more mountainous interior is conducive to planting vines, Crete's wine output is commensurate with its physical size. Nearly one-fifth of Greek wine is Cretan, and it is from Crete that many of Greece's finest dry red wines – wines that will compete with the best anywhere – could issue in coming decades.

Against all the odds, given its latitudinal position, Crete is ideal for the vine. While having extensive insolation, this most southerly of the Aegean isles enjoys a climate so mild and free of extremes that the eighteenth-century French visitor Savary was prompted to say he could not think of its climatic equal among the places where he had sojourned. The only recurrent environmental hazard facing Cretan wine-growers is the possibility of severe winds blowing off the Aegean in spring, during budding or fruit-setting. During the growing season, Crete, which is long from east to west, narrow from north to south, is cooled by sea breezes along its broader northern side, while the

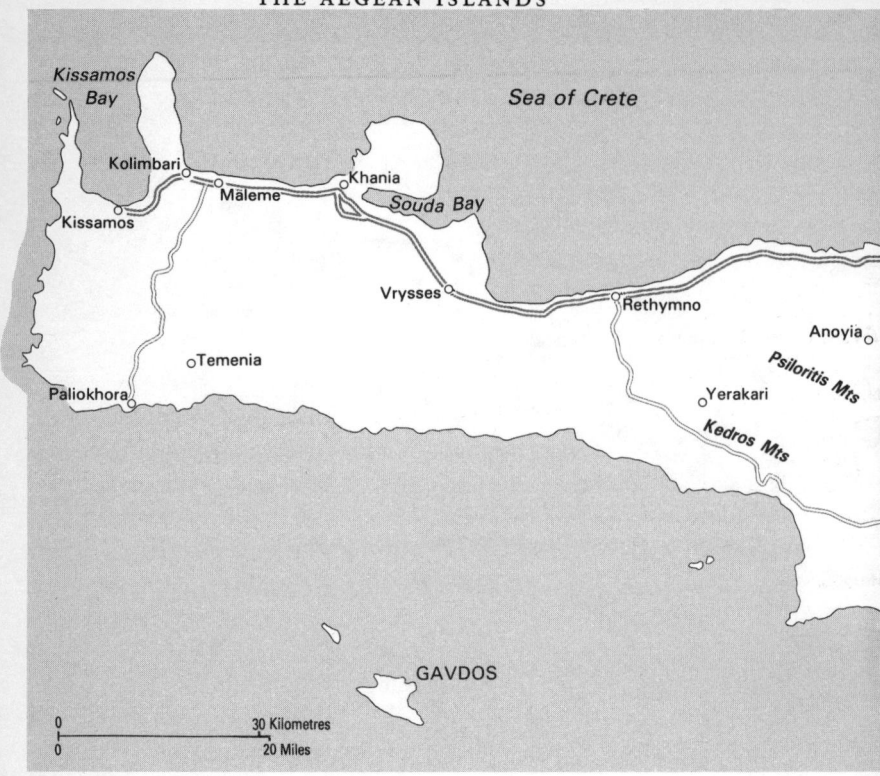

lateral extensions of Psiloritis, the Mount Ida of the ancients, provide shelter from the hot winds of North Africa. The mountains also supply plenty of water for agricultural purposes, all the way into summer too, as the snows of Psiloritis melt. The water seeps down through calcareous rock to the vineyards, and then onward again through unseen potholes, to the sea.

Crete's particularly outstanding environmental attributes have led to the development of a wine tradition second to none in all respects, including a selection of vines all its own, and more ancient than virtually any other regional tradition. Indeed, to explore the sources of the Cretan tradition is to trace the essentials of wine-growing back four millennia. Crete was certainly not among the very first places to cultivate the vine, nor even to make wine; but the remains of grapes

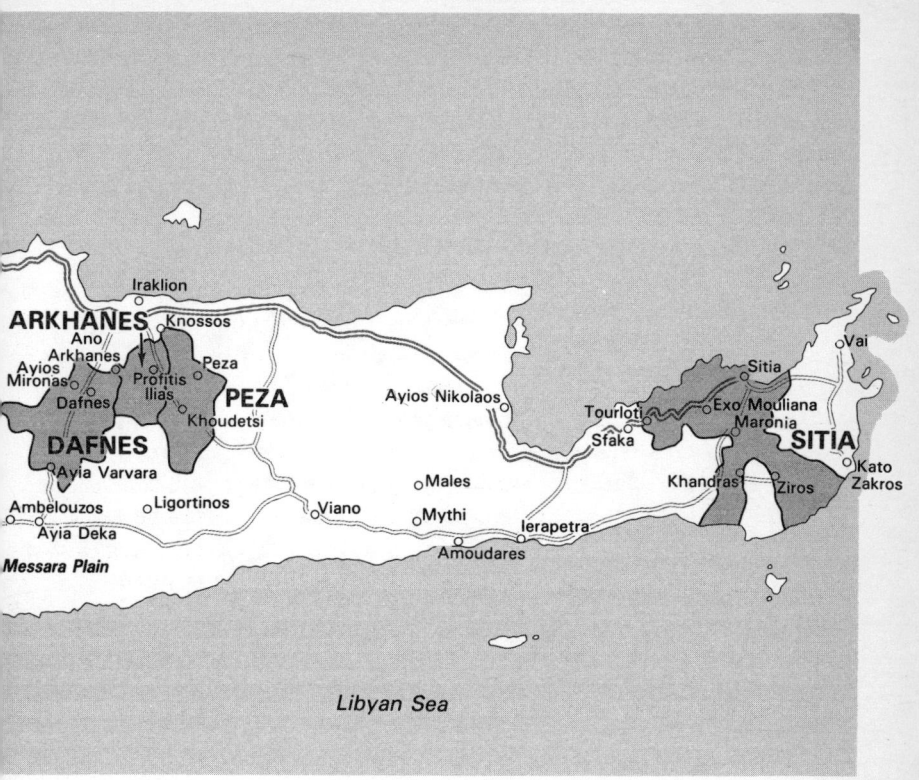

Crete

found at Kato Zakros, a site on the eastern part of the island and dating to the early second millennium BC, are the earliest conclusive evidence of systematic cultivation of grape types destined specifically for wine production. Moreover, the facilities found there for crushing the grapes indicate that Cretan, or more properly, Minoan, wine-making was technically far in advance of practice elsewhere at the time.

Following its own era of singular renown, Crete apparently was able to hold its own while progressing largely in step with innovations such as the shift to barrels. The island remained a most respected source of wine well into the modern era, even into the period of Venetian control, from the early twelfth through to the mid-seventeenth century, when Crete entered the malvasia trade (see pages 74–8). Production of that sort of wine may in no small measure account for the continuity in the island's commercial wine activity during the Ottoman centuries that followed. However, Crete's trade in wine was subsequently threatened by attempts to produce wine of malvasia type in the western Mediterranean in order to take advantage of the market Crete had created, and to be in a position to fill the gap between supply and demand, should Cretan exports dry up as a result of internal problems on the island. In fact Crete became the greatest perennial trouble spot for the Porte, thereby putting the island's reliability as a supplier in jeopardy. And although winemaking at artisan level survived intact – scenes drawn by Crete's native son Nikos Kazantzakis in *Zorba the Greek* and *Freedom or Death* give the lie to any assumption that Cretan wine tradition was obliterated by Ottoman rule – Crete's repeated insurrectionary activity held back progress in wine-making at a crucial period. The insurrection of 1896, in particular, resulted in extensive destruction of Cretan vineyards.

Crete was ceded to Greece by the Turks relatively late, in 1913. A renaissance of wine-growing on the island was prompted only in the 1930s, following a large influx of refugees from Asia Minor after the Greek–Turkish exchange of minorities agreed to in 1923. The refugees settled mostly in east-central Crete, where their initial role was largely in the spread of raisin (*soultanína*) and table grape (*rozakí*) cultivation. Nevertheless, their propensity for cooperative agricultural activities was the spur needed to revamp island winemaking. The influence of the refugees was in that way so pervasive that Cretan commercial wine-making even now remains very largely the province of cooperatives, notwithstanding the entry of several privately owned wineries. The cooperatives are likely to remain predominant far into the future as well, a prospect by no means prejudicial to the future of Cretan wine. Cretan cooperatives bring to their work a mix of enthusiasm, acumen, competence and pride, of a kind that one might be tempted to identify as specifically Cretan.

The cooperatives are seeing to the rapid extension of vineyard land, especially in the appellation of origin zones (all of which have thus far been unscathed by phylloxera), and are continuously striving to update their facilities and techniques as finances permit. Grapes are carefully separated so as to be able to offer high-quality wines, and in a couple of instances wines have been produced that, when given the time due to them in bottle, and then perhaps a 'blind tasting' as well, can make Tournefort's otherwise perhaps dumbfounding early eighteenth-century assessment far more comprehensible than might seem possible to those unacquainted with the wines of Candia. It is mostly the lack of incentive as yet to take the last step and process separately the choicest fruit of only the very best vineyards, that still keeps Crete off the topmost rung of quality in bottled dry red wine.

ARKHANES AND PEZA

Most visitors to Crete arrive at its chief town of Iraklion on the north-central coast. The scattered vineyards seen along the road south from there to Knossos might be particularly evocative of the oft-repeated aphorism that the spread of Western civilization is to be traced along the tendrils of the vine. Beyond Knossos the vines become profuse, especially after the fork in the road where one must choose between making the gradual ascent into either of two hilly, upland valleys, both of which produce exceptional wine. The westerly valley, which runs up the eastern foothills of Mount Youkhtas, within sight of Psiloritis, is that of Temenos. The villages of Ano Arkhanes, Kato Arkhanes and Skalani, as well as those of Vasilies, Ayios Silas, Profitis Ilias, and Kiparisos on the western side of Youkhtas, produce dry red wine eligible for the Arkhanes appellation of origin. Nearly 500 hectares qualify at present. The valley to the east of Temenos is that of Pedias, whose vineyards comprise the core of the Peza appellation zone for dry red and white wine. A dozen and a half villages are included in the zone: Peza, Kounavi, Mirtia, Astraki, Katalagari, Ayies Paraskies, Kalloni, Ayios Vasilios, Khoudetsi, Meleses, Astritsi and Alagni, along with Sambas further east, and Patsideros, Panorama, Damania, Metaxokhori and Kharaki further south. More than 800 hectares of vineyards in this area currently qualify for the appellation.

The gravelly, white and tan ground of the twin valleys is covered over during the growing season by a most luxurious growth of vines, some for wine, some for dessert grapes, and some for raisins, the plots for each type being laid out like a patchwork quilt. The dominant red grape of the area is the very highly regarded regional peculiarity *kotsifáli*, a variety which does well on somewhat deep clayey soils of calcareous nature. Greek wine professionals tend to liken *kotsifáli* wine to Bordeaux, which is not to draw a comparison of the variety with *cabernet sauvignon* in any strict sense. Rather, they have in mind the make-up in alcohol, acidity and extract by which *kotsifáli* wine can benefit from years of maturation in bottle, especially to the advantage of bouquet development – which will indeed occur if the wine is well made from exceptional grapes of a good year, although at the end of that time the texture and the overall feel of the best *kotsifáli* wines may be reminiscent of *nebbiolo* and *brunello*. In specifics of bouquet, however, they are quite unique.

In speaking of the *kotsifáli* in connection with Bordeaux, it also ought to be emphasized that the variety is not without tendencies that beg correction. Consequently, red wines of Arkhanes and Peza, like those of Bordeaux, have typically been made from a blend of varieties, in this case two: the dominant *kotsifáli* together with the popular southern Aegean *mandilariá* – the latter generally in a proportion of not less than 20 per cent, but not more than 40 per cent. In addition to augmenting tannin content, lowering acidity, and tempering alcoholic degree in *kotsifáli* – all to the real advantage of the wine – the *mandilariá* also deepens colour and makes it more stable, which can be a problem with varietal *kotsifáli* wine generally. Fortunately for this ideal marriage of varieties, both the *kotsifáli* and the *mandilariá* ripen in central Crete around early September.

Three commercial wineries are presently at work in the Arkhanes and Peza areas. The Archanes Wine, Olive Oil and Credit Cooperative produces about 30,000 hectolitres annually of an appellation wine called Archanes, produced from a 3:1 mix of *kotsifáli* and *mandilariá*. At Peza, about 20,000 hectolitres of red wine entitled to the appellation are produced by the Union of Producer Cooperatives of Peza, and bottled under the Mantiko label. The Union is hopeful of increasing production by half over the next ten years. Their blend of *kotsifáli* and *mandilariá* is in a ratio of about 4:1. A second local producer of appellation Peza wine is Miliarakis Brothers, who turn out about 8,000 hectolitres of it annually, produced from an undisclosed proportion of the two varieties, and marketed under the Sant'Antonio label. Qualitative comparison of the three wines is made difficult by the divergence in their barrel maturation. One would have to follow bottlings of them for some years, and none of the three is vintage-dated at present. The minimum barrel-ageing time under appellation regulations for both Arkhanes and Peza red wines is one year. But Sant'Antonio receives five to six years, compared to two to three for Mantiko and rather more than one year for Archanes.

Owing to their large production, the two cooperatives have to be in the business of selling far and wide, and being thus particularly interested in export sales have abjured the longer maturation in wood given to the wines traditionally most esteemed by the Cretans. Especially at Arkhanes, the Cooperative would like their wine to impress as 'fresh and fruity', even while they also aim for rather full body. If their Archanes succeeds in that way – and I have not thought it does – it nevertheless needs two to three years in bottle to display its character, and up to six to eight years to overcome a certain toughness to its hide. Only then will it exhibit the quality the locals boast of when asserting that Arkhanes's wine is naturally superior to that of Peza because the vineyards of Temenos reach to 600–700 metres above sea level, compared to Peza's lowly 500–600 metres. But Mantiko, too, can be quite impressive at eight to ten years of age, if one has acquired it soon after bottling and stored it oneself. Perhaps these ages do not impress Bordeaux enthusiasts, but I am speaking of aged wines that show *no* untoward manifestations whatsoever. One could expect even more from limited production Arkhanes and Peza wines, and in that regard I might usefully mention an outstanding Peza wine produced and bottled by a hobbyist wine-grower, and tasted to full satisfaction in New York just under twenty-five years later.

Although a wine of deep ruby colour, Archanes does not wear its violet on its sleeve, and actually has a latent orange cast to it even while new to the bottle. Mantiko is a shade lighter. Archanes has seemed to me the longer in finish, when aged, but Mantiko more intensely bouqueted at any age. I suppose one may weigh those respective advantages as one wishes. When bottled, Mantiko offers ample features of all that can be conjured up by the Greek term *moskhovolistó* (sweet-smelling, literally 'musk-casting'), in so far as it can be applied to dry red wines. In addition to smells of spices, this wine has an almost tropical-fruity aroma, sometimes including the smell of nearly ripe banana, which seems to me to be a *kotsifáli* trait. Also floral aromas seem to accumulate with bottle age in the case of both wines, though only to the advantage of the overall impression I have characterized as *moskhovolistó*; which tempts me to say that, at peak development, Mantiko and Archanes make what is praised in the best Burgundian noses as oriental look positively occidental instead.

However, there is more to central Crete than the casting of musk, and those who hate to see not so much the dying away of tradition, as the narrowing of the range of accepted vinous flavour, will be pleased to find that Miliarakis Brothers capture that something extra in their appellation Peza wine, Sant'Antonio. Following traditional regional practice for reserve red wine, Sant'Antonio is kept long enough for it to acquire rather distinctive flavour features which are spoken of collectively as *i yéfsi tis doúgas* (the taste of the stave). The expression implies 'over'-maturation in wood, and while it is usually used pejoratively, or at least jocularly, it can be complimentary when a certain conjunction of feel and bouquet are indicated.

The condition of *i yéfsi tis doúgas* is brought about in the first place by the phenomenon of intense insolation, common in the southern Aegean, whereby acidity in fruit that stays on the vine until fully ripe is altered in a way analogous to the malolactic, or secondary, fermentation of wines, by which malic acid is converted to the softer, less acidic tasting, lactic acid. Red wines produced from such fruit consequently do not need to undergo the malo-lactic fermentation achieved in the cellar, and desirable in northerly European wine regions to bring acidity down to levels generally felt to be more palatable. On the contrary, they need protection from it if the loss of enlivening acidity, or at least that of a kind preferred today, is to be prevented. While that has been possible in good Cretan cellars – for example, those belonging to Cretan monasteries, such as the erstwhile one of Arkadi, mentioned so favourably in some early Western travelogues – and achieved consistently in modern facilities guided by contemporary enological science, such was generally not the case under village conditions. It was therefore necessary to find a way of making a vice out of a virtue, so to speak. Hence the quest for a sound manifestation of *i yéfsi tis doúgas*. For success, a full-bodied wine of relatively high alcoholic degree is needed, in other words one that will hold up in all its essentials over the years.

At 13° alcohol, Sant'Antonio is more in keeping with traditional Cretan preferences in this respect than are the 12.5° wines of the cooperatives. While hardly lacking in acidity, it is rounded to the point that it makes overtures to flatness, and yet without compromising its health or character at all. In bouquet, Sant'Antonio exhibits something of a 180° swing away from a Peza wine like

Mantiko, as though having moved away from fresh fruit towards the essence as achieved through sun-drying. It is a kind of aromatic decay, but short of that point at which so many aromas of advanced age have crept in that it would be hard to distinguish it as Peza wine among so many other over-the-hill red wines; it all has much to do with pushing the limits of 'distinctiveness of bouquet', which perhaps occurs more often in the case of cheese, as when lovers of 'ripe' blue-veined cheeses experience difficulty in identifying advanced specimens of, say, Roquefort and Gorgonzola. That aspect of Sant'Antonio is supported and enhanced by its full body and liquorous texture. Also characteristic of Sant'Antonio is its unusual colour. Staying in barrel for as long as it does, it shows clear orange highlights, although it is none the less very dark red, darker even than newly bottled Archanes.

The red wines of east-central Crete offer an excellent opportunity to serve quality red wine at meals featuring highly flavoured pork dishes. With Archanes, try roast pork with spiced apples, or red cabbage cooked with apples; with Mantiko, hickory-smoked, slightly tangy barbecued pork can be a delight. Roast duck with raspberry sauce could also be an occasional choice, but a well-aged bottle from an outstanding bottling would go perfectly with a really well-made *mousaka*. As for Sant'Antonio, the Cretans rather appreciate it with gamy meats.

Because the valleys of Temenos and Pedias have far more vineyard land than that which yields appellation of origin red wines, other wines are also produced and bottled. Two of these, Regalo, from the Union of Peza, and Vilana from Miliarakis, are dry white wines which bear an appellation and come from the demarcated Peza area, Peza being the only one of the Cretan appellation districts that has an entitlement for white wine. The only variety authorized for appellation Peza white wine is the *vilána*, an old local type whose name dates to Venetian times and is reminiscent of the French *vilain*, going back to feudal times: *vilána* was a name given to a Cretan 'manor' of sorts. The attraction of Regalo, a soft, non-crisp wine of lightish body, is primarily in its aromatic savour when caught fresh, and not served chilled as though it were a *sauvignon blanc*. It is produced from choice *vilána* grapes and bottled without spending any time in wood; *vilána* is known to yield easily oxidized wines.

The Union of Peza's second-line red and white are 12.5° wines under the Cava 33 label (the number refers to 1933, the year the

Union was established). The red and white Cava are produced, respectively, from *kotsifáli* and a mixture of *vilána* and *rozakí*. Both are bottled at about one and a half years of age, after spending one year in oak. Red Cava 33, a rare all-*kotsifáli* wine, has an advantage for the short-term visitor in the very good quality it achieves by the time it is bottled. The Union also produces good ordinary red (*kotsifáli* and *mandilariá*), rosé (*kotsifáli*) and white (*vilána*) wines under the Logado label. In addition there is a retsina, made from *vilána* and *soultanína*, and called Ekavi after an ancient name for Crete. For its part, the Archanes Cooperative offers red (*kotsifáli* and *mandilariá*), rosé (*kotsifáli*), and white (*vilána*) wines under the Armanti label, all at 12°. As a threesome, they stand out in Greece as a second-line group of wines, and are notable for their marked regional character, particularly in their fleshy texture. Perhaps the fact that a second-line group can be so good is a true indication of the vaunted superiority of Arkhanes over Peza. Miliarakis Brothers also have a 13.3° red called Castello, made from *kotsifáli* and *mandilariá* and aged three years in barrel. Its 12.5° white counterpart, Minos Kava, is also aged in wood for three years. It is a fullish, firm and somewhat woody white made from *vilána, athíri* and *thrapsathíri*, a very old varietal combination, linked to Crete's former participation in the malvasia trade.

CLASSICAL REFLECTIONS

Inasmuch as it so obviously postdates the introduction of wooden barrels, the expression *i yéfsi tis doúgas* belongs to the modern era. Yet it may well reflect a particular outlook on the ageing of wines which the ancients shared, and which also has come down to the West at large through the term *rancio* – considered as a sensory concept, a notion of flavour, rather than as a particular wine-making process – whose epicentre is in the north-western Mediterranean basin, where Greek influence was pervasive in ancient times. *Rancio* literally means rancid, and it may be for that reason that English and French connoisseurs prefer to hear the notion alluded to in other than their native tongue. In employing the term *i yéfsi tis doúgas*, the Cretans too could be avoiding the suggestion of rancidness, but the Greeks once had exactly that word for it.

Perhaps the ancient Greeks did not want to attract bad luck by appearing to the gods as complaining of any surpluses that they might have enjoyed, but they nevertheless did not overlook qualitative changes undergone by the comestibles they were able to store:

> food prepared from new or freshly slaughtered produce – not only barley-cakes, legumes, bread, and wheat, but also flesh of animals fattened on this year's fodder, does differ in flavour from the old and is more inviting to those who experience and partake of it
> (Plutarch, *Moralia*, 'Table-talk')

They became keenly aware of the process of decay in particular, whose aromatic effects they referred to as *saprós* (putrid/rotten):

> Putridity [*saprótis*] however is a general term, applied, one must say, to anything which is subject to decay: for anything which is decomposing has an evil odour – unless indeed the name be extended to sourishness [*oxýtiti*] in wine because the change in wine is analogous to decomposition.
> (Theophrastus, *Concerning Odours*)

Indeed they had extended the word to wine, and by Theophrastus's time had built up around their notion of 'putridity' a technology for successfully ageing wines: 'there will be as much [wine] as we desire, and it shall be very [sweet-drinking], too, with no teeth in it, already grown mellow [*saprós*], marvellously aged' (Alexis, *The Dancing-Girl*, as quoted by Athenaeus in *The Deipnosophists*). 'Decay' in wine, as in all else, was attributed to the action of air – today we would say 'oxygen' – and wine, according to Plutarch, was thought 'of all things whose quality air alters . . . the most susceptible' (*Moralia*, 'Table-talk'). However, preventing wine's contact with air was not thought possible, or even desirable. The ancients' experience with olive oil, which they saw as a highly dense liquid practically impervious to air, convinced them that oil did not age well, precisely because its relative incapacity to interact with air caused its qualities to turn in on themselves, so to speak; thus oil, in Plutarch's words, gets 'stale', and not 'better', by long storage. On the other hand, some aeration might have favourable results on wine, since, as Theophrastus indicated, not *all* odours which occur in conjunction with 'decay' are necessarily noxious in and of themselves, or disagreeable to the human organism.

Ageing wine for beneficial change was seen in terms of guiding the 'decay' by controlling the wine's contact with air. The chief difficulty was presented by the porosity of the earthen jars in which wine was customarily kept:

> When our peasants are bringing corn from the country into the cities in wagons, and wish to filch some away without being detected, they fill earthen jars with water and stand them among the corn; the corn then draws the moisture into itself through the jar and acquires additional bulk and weight.
>
> (Galen, *On the Natural Faculties*)

To slow down the effects of oxygen on wine, the jars could be buried in the ground and then covered over with earth, 'so that', noted Plutarch, 'as little air [the destructive element] as possible may come into contact with them' (*Moralia*, 'Table-talk'). The ancients thus appear to have anticipated the much later corked wine bottle, and to have enjoyed a certain jar bouquet in place of our bottle bouquet. Yet even in cases where extraordinary means of slowing oxidation were used, the resultant wine was understood to have been undergoing 'decay', however slow and however slight the direct role of air, since the seeds of decay were seen as having been sown by that element in any case.

A particular kind of wine produced by calculated oxidation of some sort was that called *saprías*, whose name can be translated somewhat freely as 'rotter', although classicists usually prefer to give it as 'the mellow'. The specifics of its production are not known, but it is likely that it was aged for between ten and twenty years, since in *The Deipnosophists* ten and sixteen years are suggested as being sufficient for a 'well-aged' wine, while Pliny (*Natural History*) stated that wines meant for drinking, as opposed to cooking, appreciate in value only up to twenty years – depreciating sharply thereafter – and made no exceptions, either among Greek or Italian wines. At any rate, the fifth-century BC poet Hermippus, quoted by Athenaeus, praised *saprías* highly for such qualities of smell as we value in bouqueted older wines: 'from the mouth of its jar as it is opened, there comes a fragrance of violets, a fragrance of roses, a fragrance of hyacinth.' He may have been waxing poetic, not to say flowery, but *saprías* was clearly no 'rot-gut'.

SITIA AND DAFNES

Among its unique grape varieties Crete has one which apparently is of most considerable antiquity. Called *liátiko*, it is a red variety whose lineage goes so far back that Greek ampelographers regard one variant of it as the ancestor of the Corinthian grape used in Greece since ancient times to make currants. Its age also seems to be attested by the fact that it is planted primarily in eastern Crete, which is one of Greece's very oldest wine-making areas. The name is a shortened form of *iouliátiko*, which refers to the month of July. The term has been used generally on Crete to designate early-ripening fruit of various kinds, but the *liátiko* does in fact ripen in early July, which perhaps explains, at least in part, its popularity in eastern Crete. Dryness of atmosphere increases from west to east on the island, and consequently a very early ripening variety is appreciated in the east.

The district where the *liátiko* is predominant in vineyards is that known as Sitia, which takes its name from the harbour town of that name at the eastern end of the north coast. It is an extensive area that begins a little to the east of the point where the coastal road from Iraklion is met by the inland road coming from Ierapetra on the southern coast. The topography in the Sitia area is varied, and vineyards are found on differing types of terrain, at a range of altitude from near sea level to about 650 metres above. The hillside vineyards of the semi-mountainous country from Tourloti in the west, eastward to behind Sitia town, and then south through Maronia to Ziros, make up a zone whose wines can qualify for the Sitia appellation of origin for varietal *liátiko* red wine, dry or sweet. Presently, about 600–700 hectares of *liátiko* are cultivated at the sites belonging to the appellation, which in addition to the aforementioned ones are: Mirsini, Mesa Mouliana, Exo Mouliana, Khamezi, Katsidoni, Skopi, Akhladia, Piskokefalo, Papayiannades, Ayios Spiridonas, Khandras, Armeni, Apidi and Stavromenos. The character and quality of wine is fairly uniform in the appellation zone, with the notable exception of the mountain plateau of Agrilos, not far from the village of Exo Mouliana and above those of Mesa Mouliana and Mirsini, in the north-western strip of the appellation area. Apparently named for the clayey (*agrillódes*) earth that predominates on it, Agrilos is mentioned, in tones reserved for Le Montrachet and such, as the site of Sitian wine at its best. Presumably it was the source of that for which, as the locals tell it, Lucullus himself was a devoted customer so many centuries ago.

> The pine has been dedicated to Dionysus because it is thought to sweeten wine . . . Theophrastus attributes this effect to the heat in the soil, saying that in general the pine grows in clayey soil, and clay, being hot, matures the wine, even as it also yields the lightest and sweetest spring-water.

> (Plutarch, Moralia, 'Table-talk')

Dry red Sitian wine entitled to the appellation of origin is being produced and bottled, primarily by the Union of Agricultural Cooperatives of Sitia, which turns out about 8,000 hectolitres of it annually, maturing the wine in oak for at least two, but usually three, years before bottling. Appellation regulations call for a minimum of one year. Some grapes from Agrilos go into the Union's appellation wine, but there is no economic stimulus as yet to produce a wine only from them. Inexplicably, the label Agrilos is being used to designate the Union's second-line red and white wines of very modest quality. The only other producer who bottles is Ioannis Kokolakis, who makes about 1,200 hectolitres of appellation wine annually, marketing it after one and a half to two years in barrel. Kokolakis owns his own vineyards, but only about one-tenth of the raw material for his wine comes from them. Mostly he buys grapes from other growers having vineyards on the mountain plateaux around Khandras, Ziros and Apidi, in the southernmost part of the appellation zone. Both the Union's and Kokolakis's appellation wines, respectively at 12.5° and 12°, are marketed under a Sitia label. Neither is vintage-dated.

Sitia has no exclusive claim to the *liátiko*. The variety apparently made its way westward on the island early during the centuries of the malvasia trade, when the *liátiko* became a variety used for that sort of wine. Another area where the *liátiko* is planted widely is south-west of Iraklion, in the Dafnes region, on the northern foothills leading toward Psiloritis. The vineyards there range around 300–400 metres in elevation, and are planted mostly with white varieties, owing to the area's one-time involvement with the malvasia trade. Nevertheless, there is a good deal of *liátiko* as well. The clones of *liátiko* are different from those at Sitia, however, and tend to produce somewhat higher yields. Also, because of lower sugar content in the grapes, the red wines of Dafnes are rather lower in alcoholic degree under traditional production conditions. Only varietal red *liátiko* wine, dry or sweet, is entitled to the appellation of origin for qualifying areas of twenty villages: Dafnes, Petrokefalo, Pentamodi, Ayios Mironas, Pirgou, Siva, Kerasia, Venerato, Avyeniki, Kato Asites and Ano Asites, as well as Prinias, Ayios Thomas, Douli, Megali Vrisi, Ayia Varvara, Panasos, Yeryeri, Ano Moulia and Larani further south. At present, nearly 400 hectares of *liátiko* are planted in the appellation Dafnes zone, but no appellation wine is being produced.

The only producer-bottler in the Dafnes region is the Union of Agricultural Cooperatives of Iraklion, or Agrunion, which makes about 7,000 hectolitres annually of regional red wine that it markets under the Malvicino label. A non-vintage-dated wine of 12.5°, Malvicino is matured in cement and stainless-steel vats for at least two years before bottling. Agrunion has not had the funds to procure enough barrels to enable a worthwhile quantity of wine to qualify for appellation status by giving it the requisite one year in oak. Without the possibility of making an appellation wine, Agrunion at present also takes the liberty of mixing into Malvicino some red wine grapes other than *liátiko*, especially *mandilariá*, which gives the wine a more reddish hue than it would have otherwise. Agrunion also produces a refreshing rosé and white pair, respectively called Rodolino (*liátiko* mixed with white varieties) and Domenico (*vilána* and *rozakí*). Both take very well to chilling. A retsina (*vilána* and *rozakí*) also appears under the Domenico label. It may be questioned whether El Greco – otherwise known as Domenikos Theotokopoulos, from the vicinity of the Dafnes region – would approve of this use of his name.

The *liátiko* is a dark red variety, but gives red wine of a colour likely to astound those who behold it for the first time. It is, in a word, orange – or at least as much so as other wines are 'red', 'white' or 'rosé': 'The Superior had exquisite wines brought for us, red, white, and orange ones, cultivated on the slopes about the Monastery [of Ayios Yeoryios, near the seaside town of Ayios Nikolaos], they merited our compliments by turns' (Savary, 1788). Home-made *liátiko* wines can actually be a quite bright orange because the skins are sometimes removed early during fermentation so as to improve the quality of the brandy made from the marc. Among the bottled *liátiko* red wines, the appellation wines of Sitia are dark orange, even brownish in some of the darker-coloured bottlings, though always with just enough red to keep one from calling them tawny. Not only is no violet exhibited as such, but a quite opposite tendency towards yellow can be discernible instead. Malvicino, although not without the orange inclination, is more of a light cranberry in colour. Considering the antiquity of the *liátiko*, as well as the ancients' fascination with the relationship between fire, sun and wine, I have wondered whether *liátiko* wine is such as might have been called *pyrrós*, or 'flame-coloured'.

It can be counted an extra blessing that the utter enchantment offered the eyes by the Sitian and Dafnian wines continues into the bouquet as well. The Sitia wines of the Union and Kokolakis, which I am in favour of drinking within two to three years of their bottling, present unusual fruity aromas, sometimes including a banana-like aspect, which differs from that possibly found in *kotsifáli* wines in being reminiscent of the fully ripe fruit. Sweet-spicy smells are evident, and with a touch of piquancy, rather like mace and nutmeg compared to cinnamon. When newly bottled, the wine has sometimes reminded me of banana or walnut bread. Malvicino, a usually less bouqueted wine, seems distinguishable in smell primarily by the absence of nuances of fruit evoking equatorial images. I have on several occasions found it developing a mixed smell of nutmeg and rose with a couple years of keeping. Ample acidity and tannic astringency keep all three of the *liátiko* wines lively from initial flavour onwards. On account of their aromatic flavour and usually somewhat fleshy texture, they lean more toward lusciousness than austerity, surely befitting Lucullus's image.

The bottled *liátiko* wines are very good with plain roast pork or fresh ham, and it is worth while looking for other pork stew to go with them: for example, Hungarian-style pork goulash with Malvicino. The Sitian wines might be reserved especially for pan-fried pork chops with spiced apples, or barbecued spare ribs with tangy sauce, although with such robust dishes I would particularly recommend very new bottlings. The *liátiko* wines do not go very well with tomato, but their texture, particularly at an early age, seems to absorb the astringency of lemon easily, making them good wines for grilled pork chops or veal escalopes served with lemon wedges. They are also suited to rich Greek dishes, including *mousaká* and the most succulent versions of *pastítsio*.

KISSAMOS

In addressing Crete, wine writers of the nineteenth century did not mention dry red wines from the areas of the island that contain today's appellation of origin regions. Instead, the Cretan area whose name is particularly connected with dry reds is that of Kissamos, an area in the far west, along the northern coast. Ironically, Kissamos today seems destined to produce its typical wines ignominiously – anonymously, so to speak – for no appellation of origin is in prospect. The predicament of Kissamos wine has been brought about by certain questions pertaining to the grape variety from which it is made.

The typical wine of Kissamos, and the one identified with the name, is a dry red vinified from the *roméïko* variety, which is thought to have been brought to western Crete by the Venetians, though from elsewhere in Greece rather than from Italy. *Roméïko*, which means 'Romaic', refers to the name by which the Greeks came to call themselves after they were incorporated into the Roman Empire; the nineteenth-century traveller Pouqueville noted that the Greeks no longer called themselves 'Hellenes', but 'Romans'. Some parts of southern Greece became associated with the geographic term *Romanía*, derived from the same source. There were even Greek wines that were traded under the latter name in modern times, such as a red from the island of Zakynthos, in the Ionian Sea. Those wines, however, may have had no particular connection with the *roméïko* variety. However it reached Crete, the *roméïko* eventually spread over virtually all the western part of the island, to the point where today it covers about four-fifths of vineyard area there, or more than 2,000 hectares.

The *roméïko* is especially predominant on the low, undulating land, mostly only 100–200 metres above sea level, in the vicinity of Khania (Canea) and Souda Bay westward to the town of Kissamos (or Kastelli) at the head of Kissamos Bay, where it is planted to the near exclusion of other varieties. A major reason for the *roméïko*'s absolute supremacy is its remunerative yields, especially on low-lying areas of relatively deep soil. Also, it is a rather late-ripening variety, usually mid-September to mid-October, which offers the attraction of high sugar content in the grapes, thus assuring a high alcoholic degree in the wine. In the past, high alcohol content was considered desirable for preserving the wholesomeness of the wine as it matured in barrel prior to commercial sale. And Kissamos was most definitely a traded wine, notwithstanding the early nineteenth-century wine writer Jullien's statement, apparently based on the word of a Western visitor, that it was 'not an object of commerce' because the cost of shipping it to the port of Khania for further dispatch was prohibitive.

Greek enologists have two objections to the *roméïko* which for the time being preclude the granting of an appellation of origin entitlement, or even 'country wine' (*topikós ínos*) status, to the traditional red wine of Kissamos. One objection concerns the tendency towards relatively high yields. Although that tendency is strongly influenced by the site where the *roméïko* is planted, attempts at restriction could face difficulties. Notably, were plantings to be proscribed in the higher-yielding areas, the political wrath of winegrowers adversely affected by it would likely be incurred, inasmuch as western Crete is less developed than other parts of the island and has relatively few alternative sources of farm income. Indeed Kissamos growers have indicated a willingness to try a variety that might yield 'better' wine, but only on condition that the substitute offers yields as satisfactory as the *roméïko*.

The other objection to the *roméïko* pertains to the colour of its grapes, and that of the red wine made from them. Generally, *roméïko* grapes are of a bluish-red colour, for which reason the variety is also known as *mávro* (black) *roméïko*. However, the grapes are often considerably lighter, even pale. Bunches of them sometimes display greenish yet fully developed berries mixed among the darker, a tendency which accounts for the variety's colloquial name *loïsima*, which can be roughly translated as 'mottler'. As a result, *roméïko* grapes processed for red wine have measurably, and frequently visually, relatively little of the anthocyanin content that gives the colour usually desired for red wine. The question is not without its subjective side, however, and one might sense that the real concern of Greek enologists as regards the colour of *roméïko* wine is its saleability on the world market.

Objections to the *roméïko* notwithstanding, another voice is quietly speaking out in favour of the variety. Perhaps inspired by the good name of Kissamos wine, Greek ampelographers are out to do something about what Professor Ulysses Davides, their doyen, sarcastically refers to as 'the colour defects, so-called, of the *roméïko*'. Having worked in the Kissamos region for several years, Professor Davides is among the most knowledgeable of Greek wine professionals on the subject of the *roméïko* – far more so than any of the Greek enologists who would cast it into the Sea of Crete. He emphasizes that the variety has a great many clones, even compared with other Greek varieties notorious for their number. The clonal population exhibits significant differences in a variety of traits, ranging from yield tendency to anthocyanin content. Identifying those *roméïko* clones showing less productivity and a higher level of anthocyanins is the first step in overcoming the existing 'problems' with red *roméïko* wine, but the clonal selection programme did not get under way until after 1980. Once the preferable clones are isolated, it will be possible to spread plantings of them, and then make wine only from them, or possibly in combination with some small proportion of other varieties yielding darker red wine. Professor Davides stresses that 'modern enology can work miracles', but miracles can sometimes require financial wherewithal, and a question mark remains over this in the Kissamos region. In any case the ampelographers will have to hurry because the enologists are already mentioning such figures as a maximum of 60 per cent *roméïko* in wines eligible just for country wine status, with the rest coming from *carignan, grenache* and possibly *mandilariá*, or else solely from *carignan* and *grenache*.

It certainly must have been the variegated aspect of the *roméïko* that suggested to growers the making of variously coloured sorts of wine from it. In the Kissamos region one can virtually run the gamut of vinous colours, and all in wines made exclusively from *roméïko*. To begin with, let us note emphatically that there are reds with a perceptible violet tendency that would explain descriptions of Kissamos wine as 'claret' in nineteenth-century wine literature. If made in the rustic way, by fermenting on stalks, they can be very tannic. Rosé wines are also made from *roméïko*, but inasmuch as they are made by the same method as for red wine, though from more lightly coloured grapes, they can be quite tannic relative to what we are accustomed to in rosé. The most unusual of the coloured wines of Kissamos is a type known as *marouvás* which is an oxidized and somewhat more potent sort of *roméïko* wine that deposits much of its red colour as it ages. *Marouvás* has some similarities with sherry-type wines, and can serve well as an aperitif. Finally, dry white wines are made from the *roméïko*, probably originally to make expedient use of poorly coloured *roméïko* bunches. They tend to be rough in feel as white wines go, even when made according to contemporary white wine technique. Greek enologists report that this is due to the characteristically very high phenolic content compared with wines made from other Greek and foreign white varieties, and rather wryly note that the *roméïko* for that reason, if for no other, cannot be a candidate for sparkling wine production.

The commercial wine output of Kissamos is handled largely by the Central Union of Khania, under which four cooperative wineries operate: at Khania, Maleme, Kolimbari, and Kissamos. Additionally, the privately owned firm of Koutsourelis has been active. Both work exclusively with the *roméïko*, and produce both red and whites from it. I shall mention the whites only in passing: Clos de Creta from the Union and Kissamos from Koutsourelis. The coloured wine most likely to arouse the curiosity of visitors is the limited production Marouvas of the Union, made in a quantity of about 50 hectolitres annually, and matured in oak for four to five years before bottling. It could possibly be mistaken for Sitian wine by any but the most regionally versed eye, at least if no Sitian wine were standing next to it. However, Marouvas is yet more lightly red, and more yellow as well, than Sitian. At 14°, it is an apotheosis of gliding texture in heady, full-bodied dry wine. Some might even think of it as 'sweet' on that account, I suppose. The Union's 12° Roméïko is distinctly redder and lighter in body, and feels drier. Considerably darker than Roméïko is red Kissamos from Koutsourelis, a 13° wine aged up to five years in barrel. Even Sitian wine, entitled as it is to an appellation, is not so red – there is real violet in Kissamos – even if it is perhaps as dark in its particular way. None of the Kissamos wines are vintage-dated at this time.

MALVASIA

The renown of Cretan wine may be said to have reached its zenith in modern times, for it was while the island was under Venetian control that its name spread farthest among wine-drinking countries. The vehicle for Crete's reputation then was the wine known as malvasia, or malmsey, a type of sweet wine that became a major export from the southern Aegean to Western Europe in the thirteenth century, and which remained important until the nineteenth. Although Crete was not the original source of wine called by that name, it later became the most significant producer and shipper – so significant in fact that some Western visitors to the Aegean came away with the mistaken impression that Crete was the only source of it.

Greek malvasia wines have been disparate as regards both their place of origin and their preparation. With reference to geographic origin, it is to be noted particularly that although the 'malvasia' name itself refers to a specific place, not all wine called by that name was actually grown there. The name comes from the town called Monemvasia, founded in the late sixth century by the Byzantines, and situated on an islet appended to the coast of the south-eastern Peloponnesos, due west of the Cycladic island of Milos. Vines were cultivated on the shore of the mainland opposite, and documents of the thirteenth century show that the wines produced there were traded under the name 'Monemvasios'. On Venetian tongues the town's name was transformed into 'Malvasia' and applied to the wines as well. Because of its key position between East and West, Monemvasia became something of an *entrepôt*, and shipped west-ward wine similar to its own that had originated elsewhere in the Aegean. Consequently all wine of that type exported from there was called 'malvasia' by Western traders, and their 'appellation' made its way back to the various places producing it. Prominent among those were Crete, Santorini, Paros, Tinos, Rhodes, and even northerly Khios. Some early travellers mistakenly considered the malvasia name to be derived from Ariousia, via 'Arvisia' and similar corrup-tions of the name of that famous Khiote wine area.

The commercial importance of Monemvasia began to decline around the end of the fourteenth century, when the West converted to types of ship that could not be safely accommodated in the harbour. Local wine production fell off as a result, and was sharply curtailed following the occupation of the Peloponnesian shore by the Ottomans in the late fifteenth century, which occasioned the departure of many inhabitants; by the time Thomas Wyse paid a visit in the mid-nineteenth century, the local folk knew nothing of malmsey. Crete, still under Venetian control, took over as the trade centre for malvasia, and also became by far the largest producer-supplier. The malvasia name continued to be used in spite of the geographic shift, and was actually reinforced by the circumstance that the area to the south-west of Iraklion producing the most, and by some reports the best, Cretan malvasia had become known as Malevizi, a name which may have related either to the area's past involvement with malvasia production or to the nearby fortified position that the Venetians dubbed *mal vicino*.

From the point of view of viti-viniculture, too, malvasia wines have historically shown some considerable variation. As with geographical provenance, however, parameters can be specified. Malvasia has usually been sweet or semi-sweet wine, but produced by varying methods. The super-maturation of grapes on the vine was probably the typical means of augmenting sugar content in the must. However, no concrete evidence rules out the possibility that harvested grapes were also dried in the sun. The must may occasionally have been cooked as well. Certainly that technique was known in ancient times, and at some places on Crete malvasia was cooked a little prior to being shipped, with the intention of temporarily stabilizing it, as Greek malvasia was *not* a fortified wine, at least not during the heyday of the trade. Not all malvasia was sweet, however. Venetian documents relating to Crete indicate that a dry kind of malvasia, *malvasia garba*, was known, if perhaps only on Crete; in 1553 the traveller Pierre Belon related that usage of the term *garba*, which he gallicized as *garbe*, equated to the French terms *rude* (astringent) and *verd* (tart).

The grape varieties used for malvasia have also been various. The diversity is particularly apparent in the fact that while malvasia wines have generally been white, a red kind is also known. Yet it is in the matter of varietal composition that the unifying theme of Greek malvasia wines manifests itself. For the fact is that the varieties upon which the wines have been based all have distinct varietal aroma, though not of the 'aromatic' muscat family; old Greek and Venetian sources differentiate malvasia from muscat wines, although the two types were confused by some early Western visitors. Instead, the varieties for malvasia are of 'semi-aromatic' type: the white *monemvasiá, aïdáni áspro, athíri, thrapsathíri, vilána, takhtás* and *triferá*; and the red *liátiko, ladikinó* and *mávro aïdáni*. The multiplicity of non-muscat varieties used for malvasia accounts for, and is verified by, the disparity among non-muscat vines now cultivated in Western Europe, but originally brought from Greece, that bear names mentioning malvasia.

Typically, Greek malvasia wines have been based on a mixture of two or three of the named semi-aromatic varieties, possibly with still others, including both non-aromatic and aromatic (muscat) sorts, used to a minor extent. Etymological evidence substantiating the mixing of varieties is manifest in two old colloquial terms from the southern Aegean areas connected with malvasia, *logádo* and *xenólogo*; their root is in the ancient verb *légo*, meaning to gather, which has given rise to a number of words suggesting variousness of kind, in the sense of a collection or assortment, much as in the case of the *loïsima* synonym of the *roméïko* grape variety. On Crete, the term *logádo*, connoting 'of assorted kind', was used to describe wine of diverse varietal origin, and also a vineyard planted with several grape varieties other than the primary ones of a site, such vineyards usually being the source of *logádo* wines. On Santorini, the term *xenóloga*, connoting 'odd kinds', is used to distinguish the diverse varieties – 'odds and ends', as it were – other than the two grape varieties mostly used for wine-making on the island, while the very closely related term *xenólogo* was formerly used as an alternative name for malvasia, since the *xenóloga* varieties were the source of that wine.

Vineyards were usually planted with the intended mix for malvasia in mind. Thus, although the varietal mixture for malvasia has ever been a movable feast, it has followed a pattern from place to place. That circumstance accounts for the otherwise seemingly haphazard varietal composition found in some vineyards of the southern Aegean today, above all in the Cyclades. In central Crete, malvasia has usually been produced from a mix of *athíri, thrapsathíri* and *vilána* (one might in this context compare the contemporary Cretan wine Minos Kava to the *malvasia garba* of old); in eastern Crete, a mix of *thrapsathíri* and *takhtás* was typical; in the Cyclades, it was usually some proportion of *monemvasiá, aïdáni áspro* and *athíri*. A notable exception to the habit of varietal mixture has been red malvasia produced from the *liátiko* variety, which must necessarily be vinified as a fully varietal wine, since the *liátiko* ripens too early to have companions in the vat.

The varietal composition of the malvasia wines, being founded mostly on very old Aegean types, admits the possibility that the same kinds of wine as some of the non-Monemvasiote wines which came to be traded as 'malvasia' may actually have been in production since long before their acquisition of that name. However, that is less likely in the case of those made in the Cyclades largely from *monemvasiá*, the 'malvasia' grape proper, a variety that almost certainly spread from the south-eastern Peloponnesos just because of intentions to imitate the wine first called 'malvasia'.

In this century malvasia has so receded in importance in Greece that it is now of no commercial significance. Since the Second World War and the subsequent population exodus from the southern Aegean area, malvasia wine has also lost ground in the living folk tradition. Indeed, even the tradition of the wine's name, which is *malvazía* in Greek, has been fading from popular memory along with the wine itself. Yet there is no compelling reason for the absence of bottled Greek malvasia on the world wine market. The southern Aegean still has a capacity to produce it commercially, especially red malvasia from Crete, which may have been the only place where much of the red kind was formerly made. For that matter, both the region of Sitia and that of Dafnes are entitled to produce appellation of origin sweet red wine, unfortified or fortified, exclusively from the *liátiko*. But where are the Luculluses today to demand it?

GASTRONOMIC NOTES

Kazantzakis's scenes of Crete can undermine stereotypical images of Aegean agriculture and cuisine: for example, the pig seems to be in constant evidence. There are those unforgettable scenes from *Freedom or Death* in which those attending Captain Michalis's several-day wine orgy are plied with *loukániko* (pork sausage), or that from *Zorba the Greek* in which the freshly neutered pig seems to have a bestial comprehension of the nature of the delicacy being enjoyed in the farmyard by his owner and the guests. Crete has in fact appreciated pork since remote antiquity – and has always managed to enjoy a good supply of it, thanks to an abundance of foodstuffs such as acorns with which to feed the creatures. Some unusual preparations of pork are to be found, such as baking it and returning it to the oven with a yogurt sauce.

The spices used in Cretan cooking can be unusual compared to the rest of the Aegean. On the one hand Crete has held on to some traditional Greek flavourings for meat dishes, like coriander and the more unusual caraway ('hare stewed with fresh onions and caraway seeds', *Freedom or Death*). On the other hand it has a particular penchant for exotic spices, and perhaps black pepper most of all. Crete was introduced to Eastern spices earlier than most of the rest of Greece, and millennia before the Ottomans arrived with their wrongly supposed all-pervasive influence on Greek cookery. Moreover, the spices are used in combinations that mark the island dishes as different even when they are otherwise of generic Greek type. Indeed some Cretan preparations could, if encountered blindly, be identified as dishes from further east than Crete.

Crete grows many fruits and vegetables, and is well known for a number of them both in Greece and abroad, but perhaps most of all for its *rozakí* table grapes, especially those from the eparchy of Iraklion, and citrus fruits, particularly the mandarins of the Khania plain. As in other parts of Greece, the natives also have special praise for certain local fruits, some of which are available only in relatively small quantity. Particular mention might be made of the chestnuts of Kissamos, the cherries of Yerakari, in the eparchy of Rethymno, and the muscat grapes of Temenia, in the Sfakia district of south-western Crete. Temenia is also known for its muscat wine. The island claims the quince as its very own: its Greek name is *kydóni*, and the ancient name of Khania, where it mostly grows, was Kydonia. The ancients used quince in their cooking, even with meat dishes, and perhaps especially with game, a habit which has not been entirely forgotten by Cretans of the present day. Another curiosity of Cretan horticulture is the island's banana trees, which grow mostly along the south-eastern coast, and produce a dwarf banana (greatly disparaged by the Athenians).

The olive tree is grown nearly all over Crete, but the island oils and table olives are generally not counted amongst the foremost of the Aegean. Nevertheless, some locales of central Crete (Vasilies, Viano) and eastern Crete (Sfakia, Ayios Stefanos) are very well regarded for their oil, while Apokorono, as the area around Khania is called, is known for a speciality oil, *agourólado*, produced from unripened olives. The eparchies of Iraklion and Lasithi also have good eating olives, especially at Vasilies in the first instance and Males in the second. The mountain plateau of Nida, by Psiloritis, provides an unusual small black olive.

The cheeses of Crete earn marks as first-rate, and fortunately some types are widely available commercially. Cow's-milk cheeses from Ambelouzos and Ayia Deka, above the plain of Messara in south-western Iraklion, are well known. Among ewe's-milk cheeses, those of Ligortinos in south-eastern Iraklion, Zenia in north-western Lasithi, Males and Mythi in south-western Lasithi, and Ziros in south-eastern Lasithi, are especially sought. The semi-hard ewe's-milk *kefalotýri* and soft *myzíthra* cheeses of Yerakari, produced in caves in the Kedros Mountains, as well as Anoyia's goat's-milk *anthótyro* ('blossom-cheese'), have special reputations. Both places are in the east of Rethymno. Cretan yogurt is also generally praised, but particularly that of Vrysses, in the eparchy of Khania.

Game is plentiful in the numerous mountainous areas of Crete, and the same is true of fish in the lesser populated parts of coastal areas. However, the Kedros Mountains are especially abundant in hare, partridge and wild pigeons, while the areas of Paliokhora and Vaï, respectively in the far south-west and far north-east of the island, yield plentiful fish, especially mullet (*lethrínia*) and sea bream (*fangriá*) at Vaï.

The islet of Gavdos, Greece's southernmost possession, lying south of the Sfakia district of Crete, affords greatly prized sheep, fed on cedar fruit and briny vegetation. The Gavdian barley bread called *pakhoúda*, made of only partially ripened barley, is very much appreciated for its special flavour, and may conceivably be a Minoan recipe.

4

Santorini

Barren, waterless, and windswept is the earth of Santorini. Because of that, even its production per hectare is small. However, all of its products without exception (perhaps because they are dry-farmed or 'on account of the volcanic nature of its earth') are remarkable and famous. But first and best is its wine: Santorinió krasí *by name.*
Filipos Katsipis, 'From the Chronicle of Our Plain' (in *Santoríni*, ed. M. Danezis), 1971.

Situated along the northern rim of the Sea of Crete, about 70 miles north of Iraklion, is a crumb of land which is arguably the most remarkable vineyard in all the Dionysian realm – Santorini, or Thira.

A visitor might well expect Santorini to produce extraordinary wine, for nothing at all about the place partakes of the ordinary. A crescent of cliffs, which looks as though it had been hacked out with one fell swoop of an Olympian axe, walls in the island's bay on the north, east and south, while the islet of Thirassia is a barrier along the north-west. The bay itself is unusual, being a caldera and harbouring a dormant volcano. Santorini's appearance and nature owe their origin to the cumulative effects of the catastrophic volcanic activity that has overwhelmed it several times since the ancient era. While some consider that Santorini may be the legendary Atlantis, there is no question but that an eruption of a former volcano on the island around 1500 BC, which is thought to have been the largest volcanic eruption in recorded history, precipitated the decline of the Minoan civilization by force of the destruction it wrought on Crete. Other major volcanic eruptions and earthquakes have struck since. Notably, in 1649 and 1650 a great frequency of strong seismic activity culminated in the appearance of a volcano out of the sea about 3–4 miles to the north-east of Santorini. Sending forth exhalations of igneous material and sulphurous smoke, the volcano coloured the sea a bright green with the dust of the spewed debris, and clouded even far-off Constantinople. The various eruptions have added to Santorini layers of volcanic material with which the island's fruits may be infused, and in effect dictated to the inhabitants that the very essence of Santorini should be their wines. The result is emphatically, as one travelled Santoriniote wine-grower says without the least exaggeration: 'Santorini's wines cannot be compared to any others in Greece or in Europe. They are entirely "of their own kind".'

The vineyards of Santorini do not file down from an Etna-like volcanic summit. The one-time peak was blown off in the eruption of 1500 BC that left the caldera. Instead, the island's cultivated area, including its vineyards, sprawls out across a plateau that slopes from about 300 metres above sea level on the west, where the multi-coloured, nearly perpendicular cliffs ring the caldera, to sea level on the east, where Santorini's black stone beaches are found. The ground itself is perhaps the most bizarre to be seen at any wine site, and can be likened to the mock-up of the moon's surface on display at the National Air and Space Museum in Washington, DC. The generally unseen base of chalk and shale has been covered over by ash, lava and smashed pumice stone, so that one might imagine, in looking at the ashen greyness of the vineyards, that the vine could be made to yield fruit on the surface of the moon, if only there were sunlight, oxygen and a drop of water. Owing to the special needs for nutriment arising from these environmental circumstances, the spacing of vines, at 2–2.5 metres apart, is more or less double that found in most of Greece. And yet the plant is nevertheless stressed to the limit.

Winds have blown so forcefully over Santorini since 1500 BC – the olive tree, which thrived until then, has ever after been able to grow only in a few sheltered places – that the inhabitants developed a practice of training the low-lying vines into the form of a basket, actually called a *stefáni* (crown), to assure survival in the winds during the fifteen to twenty years of growth the vines require before they can support themselves. After that period, the practice can be discontinued in the depressions the Santoriniotes call 'amphi-theatres', but in raised areas, which are particularly threatened by wind, the 'crown' is maintained throughout the life of the plant. The winds also tend to dry up what moisture might otherwise be taken up from the insular atmosphere. The only water the plants have is that released at night by the island's layer of china clay, which manages to absorb some moisture from the air. Equally important during the very warm ripening period is the preclusion by the winds of condensation on the grapes themselves. In this way acidity in the fruit, far from being lost, on the contrary fully keeps up with the mounting sugar content, rarely surpassed elsewhere in the Aegean.

The leading grape variety of Santorini is the white *asýrtiko,* which accounts for about 70 per cent of vineyard area. It is traditional only on Santorini, which is a rather unusual occurrence in Greek viticulture and would seem to lend credence to suppositions that it arrived from abroad in recent centuries, although its exact derivation is not known. One old Santoriniote explanation is that the *asýrtiko* arrived from the Jerez region of Spain, but this has not been the subject of systematic ampelographic research. The lore on this point presupposes that the variety's name was derived from the Greek version of the name 'sherry' or *sérri: asýrtiko* would signify 'sherrian' in that case. Yet it is also possible that the Jerez/'sherry' region may have been referred to by those who gave the *asýrtiko* its name because the relatively tannin-rich white wines oxidize easily. When *asýrtiko* grapes are high in sugar content their always high content of aromatic substances soars, and they can then be elaborated to produce unfortified wine analogous to sherry. The *asýrtiko* ripens on Santorini in mid-September and is remarkable for its cooperation with a native 'super-strain' of yeast in producing wines of as high as 18° natural alcohol.

Another 20 per cent of Santorini's vineyards are planted with the black *mandilariá,* which can succeed unusually well under the local conditions. The remaining 10 per cent is taken up by some forty other sorts of grapes, all of which are used more or less frequently in wine-making, but most of all the whites *athíri* and *aïdáni áspro* (the latter surely must be the *edáni* grape mentioned by the lexicographer Hesychius around the fifth century AD) which are often significant in a varietal mixture. The island's varietal make-up heavily favours the making of white wine, which in fact comprises nearly 80 per cent of Santorini's production. Largely in consideration of that, Santorini, including Thirassia, is an authorized appellation of origin zone for qualifying dry or sweet white wines produced from the varieties *asýrtiko, athíri* or *aïdáni áspro,* in any combination, or individually, although fully varietal *athíri* or *aïdáni áspro* wine is most unlikely to be made.

'The Santoriniotes', wrote the eighteenth-century resident French priest Abbé Pègues, 'well understand how to fabricate their wine.'

Their cellars must have afforded them the chance to observe and consider the matter. Traditionally, Santorini's wines have been made in small cellars hewn out of the pumice stone known locally as *áspa*. Structures almost identical to the cellars were used for animal quarters as recently as the nineteenth century, and were very likely once indistinguishable from human dwellings. The overlap of purpose can be understood from the very sound resistance such structures have to earthquakes, and from the stability of temperature they provide. *Áspa* structures are cool in the warm weather, while requiring no heating in the cold months, and so are quite capable of providing a very healthy environment for the long maturation of wines to which nature guarantees abundant alcohol, acidity and extract. The traditional cellars are now going out of use in favour of more modern facilities, however.

The most usual type of traditional Santoriniote wine is that which goes by the generic name *broúsko*, a name acquired during the time of Venetian rule on the island, from the thirteenth to the mid-sixteenth century. *Broúsko* may be white, red or rosé. *Asýrtiko* supplies by far the greater part of the must for white *broúsko*, which is expected to have an incipient brownishness that the native writer Katsipis describes as 'cinnamony'. However, other white varieties are included as well, especially the *aïdáni áspro* because of the esteem in which its aromatic qualities are held. For red *broúsko*, the *mandilariá* is most important, but other black and red varieties are also used, and often some *asýrtiko* is added; not all Santoriniote reds conform to Greek conceptions of 'black' wine. Rosé wine, of which there is only a small quantity, is made from a mix of white with black and red grapes, mostly *asýrtiko* and *mandilariá*, but in a proportion much to the detriment of red colour in the wine. In the traditional Greek eye the rosé may none the less qualify as 'reddish'; *erythróxantho*, literally 'red-blonde', is the term usually heard on Santorini.

Under traditional conditions, it has been customary to collect the bulk of the grapes for *broúsko* wines in the crushing basins of the cellars for two to four days before wine-making gets under way. Traditionally crushed by foot – today's major commercial producers generally use mechanical equipment – these grapes go into the vats to ferment with the skins and stems for an extended period. The musts typically ferment out to about 16°, but 17° is not uncommon. Because of the long contact of the juice with the skins after harvesting, the wines thus produced are somewhat astringent – even the white wines, since the *asýrtiko* is relatively tannic. The high level of overall non-sugar extract content, in combination with high acidity, also makes them slightly coarse, and all the more so if they happen to be made from later pressings of the grapes. This is how these wines acquired the *broúsko* name, which signifies 'rough'. Some Santorini-otes maintain that maturation in barrel over several years is tradition-ally considered indispensable for *broúsko* of any colour, but they are indicating an exceptional one. In practice, traditional *broúsko* wine accorded a lengthy barrel maturation is usually made from free-run must and destined for family consumption and preferred customers. However, whether matured this way or not, *broúsko* wines can be of resounding excellence, if even then unlikely to attract every favourable descriptive wine term currently in vogue. Santorini is that special.

Another type of Santoriniote dry wine is the one traditionally called *nyktéri*, a name which may be best translated as 'the night one'. The late nineteenth-century Cycladic explorer James Bent related that it takes its name from the expression *tis nyktós* or 'of the night', the grapes for it being picked before sunrise, so as to enhance flavour. The thinking behind such a practice would seem to be a relic of ancient times, when apparently considerable attention was paid to the time of day at which edibles were to be gathered or hunted, the object being to enjoy peak flavour. The tendency was so wide-spread then that it moved Horace to wryness: 'After this he informed me that the honey-apples were red because picked in the light of the waning moon. What difference that makes you would learn better from himself.' Lucian quotes Eucrates telling of a vintage season, when 'passing through the farm at midday, I left the labourers gathering the grapes' (*The Lover of Lies*), from which we might assume that daytime collection was the norm and anything else extraordinary. Greek enologists today know for a fact that dawn harvesting of grapes in the Aegean generally is desirable if fresher-tasting, less oxidation-prone dry white wines are to be produced. Still, Bent's explanation of *nyktéri*'s name is refuted by present-day Santoriniotes. Their explanation is that the choice grapes used are processed on the same day they are picked – a practice also recommended by the enologists – which entails working into the night in the cellars. Indeed the Aegean idiom 'to do *nyktéri*' means 'to work late'.

Nyktéri is always white. Its typical varietal make-up is *asýrtiko* with admixture of *aïdáni áspro* and *athíri*. As with white *broúsko*, fermentation is on stems and skins, but in this case same-day processing of the select grapes results in a colour which Katsipis has described as 'whiter even than retsina'. Or as another old-timer has expressed it, *nyktéri* 'shouldn't have colour'. These descriptions are meant to indicate yellow colour devoid of any brownish nuance, and that seems to be the essential visual expectation for *nyktéri*, in spite of the five years or more of barrel maturation regarded as necessary if the wine is to have been worth the extra effort in harvesting and vinifying. Generally, *nyktéri* is somewhat lower in alcohol than a white *broúsko* would be under traditional production conditions, because of the speedy processing of the grapes, but 15° is usual.

Santorini's uniqueness is vivid in its ultra-sweet *visánto*, a wine that has carried its Italian name only since Venetian times. Its tradition is doubtlessly far older. In age-old fashion, the well-ripened grapes are spread in the sun for one to two weeks, according to seasonal conditions, which is probably what caused the Venetians to think of *vin santo*. After the grapes have darkened to a state called 'half-baked' (*misopsiména*), the grapes are crushed by foot. Fermentation is on skins and stems. Owing to the exceptionally high sugar content, the must undergoes a very slow initial fermentation, lasting about fifty days. A decade in barrel is quite usual for maturation, but even then a *visánto* reaches only 8–9° alcohol. *Visánto* can be white, red or rosé, but Santoriniotes solidly grounded in their wine-making tradition are agreed in specifying that the basic island varieties, *asýrtiko* and *mandilariá*, are the foundation for true *visánto* wine, and this is confirmed by Pègues's eighteenth-century report. Depending on the colour of the intended *visánto*, white (*áspro*) or black (*mávro*) *aïdáni* usually has a role as well. Sometimes *athíri* grapes, again white or black, the latter sort being called *mavrathíri*, are also included.

Perhaps because neither all Santoriniotes nor all of their customers ordinarily cared to have a wine as sweet as *visánto*, a less sweet offshoot also developed in island tradition. Colloquially called *médzo*, from the Italian term *mezzo* (medium), but more formally referred to as *imíglyko* (semi-sweet), for the sake of other Greeks, that wine is produced in either of two ways. Must of fresh grapes and 'half-baked' ones may be mixed half-and-half, or all of the grapes may be 'baked' half as long as for *visánto*. Alcohol is usually at 15–16°.

Another traditional sweet wine is *malvazía*, or *malavazías* as it is called on Santorini. It differs from *visánto* with respect both to varietal make-up and treatment of the grapes. Unlike *visánto*, a true *malvazía* is based on varieties other than *asýrtiko* and *mandilariá*, and always several of them. Indeed, *malvazía* was once also known on the island as *xenólogo*, a term connoting 'from various kinds', much as *xenóloga* is the term by which the island's many minor varieties are collectively called. Another divergence from *visánto* is that the formation of high sugar content in the grapes is achieved mostly or entirely by super-maturation on the vine. If sun-drying is used, it is only for a minority of the grapes, and usually for *aïdáni áspro* in particular, the must from which is subsequently added to the wine of the other grapes. The wine obtained in either case is a fully sweet one, but always less sweet and of higher alcohol degree, 15–16°, than *visánto*. However, almost nothing is heard of *malvazía* on Santorini now. A very few wines which are substantially just that are still produced, but post-Second World War reports on *visánto* by non-Santoriniote wine professionals suggest a tendency towards fusion of the *visánto* and *malvazía* concepts in the mind of some Santoriniote wine-growers in recent decades. It is notable particularly in the use of the island's less usual varieties as the basis for wines produced more like a *visánto* than a *malvazía*, and therefore called *visánto*. Also, true *malvazía* is occasionally called *visánto* if some of the harvested grapes have been sun-dried.

At present, Santorini's commercial bottlers are also facing pressure to accommodate the singular nature of true Santoriniote wine to more conventional tastes. The dilemma in this 'internationalization' of Santorini wine, which lies in making the accommodation without forfeiting the remarkable character of the best traditional wines, is especially acute with respect to dry wines. On account of the high alcohol degree of the traditional wines – *broúsko* and *nyktéri* – Santorini's bottlers found it difficult to persuade outsiders to try them as mealtime beverages more than once. Visitors would sample them, but found them 'deliciously treacherous', to quote one comment, since their vibrant acidity and unmatched aromatics effectively throw a deceptive mask over the wines' potency, as the unsuspecting newcomers subsequently discovered. Consequently, the dry wines now produced for bottling are mostly what might be thought of as modified *broúsko*: wine made along the general lines for *broúsko*, but with earlier harvesting of the grapes so as to produce wine of restrained alcoholic degree. In dry white wines in particular, the traditional distinction between *broúsko* and *nyktéri* seems to be eroding as well. Needless to say, perhaps, the bottlers, who in any case generally evince little interest in appellations of origin, do not all share the viewpoint of those professionals at the Greek Wine Institute who argue that appellation regulations for Santorini should be revised to require a minimum of 15° alcohol for dry white wine.

The bottling of wine on Santorini is something of an innovation, and does not go back much before the 1970s, although sporadic attempts were made in earlier decades. The perseverance of the bottlers at this time, however, is of special importance because it offers the chief hope of bringing a halt to the ongoing abandonment of the Santorini vineyard. In the mid-nineteenth century, when Russian demand for Santorini's wine was at fever-pitch, around 4,000 hectares were producing. After Russian demand subsided early in this century, an alternative to wine-growing on Santorini appeared in the form of a dwarf tomato plant that gives a paste of extraordinary flavour, so that without the aid of phylloxera, vineyard area had fallen back to about 3,400 hectares by 1950. More recently the tomato-processing industry has sharply retrenched, and yet wine-growing, far from taking up the slack in the island's economy, has continued on an increasingly rapid downward spiral, owing to emigration, the lure of the tourist industry and rising labour costs. Currently, only about 1,500 hectares of vines are producing. Some Santoriniotes direly predict the eventual disappearance of vines altogether if labour costs continue to gain on wine prices, a sad prospect indeed for the island that has yielded the earliest pictures of clusters of wine grapes of modern type, on an earthen vessel dating to about 1500 BC.

Competition between bottling wineries could possibly reverse the deteriorating profitability of vine cultivation. Six wineries are currently producing and bottling. The largest is that of the Union of Agricultural Cooperatives of Santorini Products ('Santo'), which until very recently had confined itself to wine expressly made for blending purposes. In the mid-1980s it undertook the production of wines for bottled sales, beginning with a threesome of red, white and rosé wines of 13°, all on the Vedema label; *'vedéma'*, another term left over from Venetian times, is the island word for 'vintage'. A better white, three years old and of 14°, was marketed on the Irini label. A dry white appellation white of 14° was put out in 1987.

Called Santorini, it is made from *asýrtiko* (80 per cent), *aïdáni áspro* (10 per cent), and *athíri* (10 per cent). It was initially produced in a quantity of less than 100 hectolitres. Altogether, the Union produces about 40,000–50,000 hectolitres of wine annually, of which only about 20 per cent is being bottled. Future plans envisage a complete refurbishing of the winery, and a considerable expansion of bottling activity, with budgetary aid from the EEC. At present, the Union has no barrels, and matures its wines in cement tanks.

The Koutsouyanopoulos Brothers own the largest of the privately run bottling wineries on Santorini. It is a family wine business dating back to 1886, though only to 1974 in bottling. Grapes are bought in from numerous island wine-growers, but about 10 per cent comes from the family's vineyards. The winery produces 4,500–5,000 hectolitres of wine annually, of which three-quarters is white. That bottled as Volcan is three-year-old white *broúsko* of the new sort, while that called Lava has only one year in barrel. These are excellent white wines of fullish body, even if it is 'too much to say that there is an eruption in every bottle', as one traveller said of some other Santorini wines a few years back. Koutsouyanopoulos produce no *visánto* or other sweet wine, in line with their stated intent to be geared to tourists' tastes, which they have divined to be for the dry as well as the tamely alcoholic. All of the Koutsouyanopoulos wines are in the range of 12° alcohol.

The Markezinis winery, located in Messaria, has been bottling since 1971 – the family has been in wine since 1827 – and produces about 1,500 hectolitres annually. About 80 per cent of the wine is white, the best of it thus far having been Santinos white, a somewhat amber, nascently pinkish *broúsko* in the new fashion (12.2°), with fullish body. Despite the winery's emphasis on white wine, its outstanding products have been dry red and rosé wines from the *mandilariá*: Santinos red (12.2°) and Cava Atlantis rosé (13°), both produced from free-run must. The latter wine was to be the forerunner of a series of reserve white, rosé and red wines that should be very well worth the small premium that will be asked, if one judges by the rosé, which takes rosé wine to previously undreamt-of heights, though at the expense of the 'lightness' some seek in this type of wine. The plain Atlantis series has been the winery's line of lesser-quality and lower-alcohol wines. Considering Markezinis's knack for spotting excellent *mandilariá* grapes, it is to be regretted that no red *visánto* is produced at his winery, but he personally does not relish *visánto* of any colour.

Canava Roussos is another old family operation, dating back to 1836; *kánava* is the Santoriniote term for 'cellar'. Based in the seaside village of Kamari, Roussos has been bottling since 1974, producing 500–600 hectolitres annually of various wines, none of which is in quantities of more than a few hundred litres each in the year of production. About 60–70 per cent of the raw material comes from the family's vineyards. Roussos is for the most part a stickler for tradition, right down to having the grapes crushed by foot, at least in so far as traditional wine types are concerned. The top products of his winery, Nykteri and Visanto, attest to the value of this practice, though I would not necessarily attribute their quality to the use of feet in particular! Roussos's flights of fancy also tend to be inspired by tradition, as in the case of a sweet red Mavrathiro, a 15° wine produced from sun-exposed *mavrathíri* and *mandilariá* in about equal proportions, and matured in barrel for more than a decade before bottling. Canava Roussos wines were the first of the island to appear with vintage dates.

The smallest of Santorini's bottling wineries is that of the Venetsanos Brothers, located in the village of Megalo Khorio. They have been bottling since 1970, but the family has been involved in the wine trade since the 1840s. About 500 hectolitres of wine are bottled annually under the Ven-San label. Nearly 400 hectolitres of it is white *broúsko* (loose definition) and *nyktéri*. White *imíglyko* wines are also produced. Even the white *broúsko* stays in barrel for almost a decade, emerging with exceptional flavours typical of the style, with the exception that, again, at around 12°, the sensations are not the most traditional for *broúsko*. The view of the elderly Venetsanos brothers, however, is that what is central to the Santoriniote tradition of *broúsko* is not a specific degree of alcohol, but rather the method of collecting the grapes, a fermentation on skins and stems, and an appropriate maturation of the wine. These, they say, are what gives the wine its requisite and inimitable aromatic character.

Most recently, a winery has been erected on the island by the Boutari firm of Macedonia. Its production in the future is likely to be second only to that of the Union in quantity, although its first bottling, in 1988, from the 1987 vintage, was of a minor quantity of white appellation wine produced on a trial basis. It was made entirely from *asýrtiko*, and marketed under a Santorini label.

As can be gleaned from this survey of Santorini's bottled wine output, the great majority is dry white wine. Just about any individual wine could be highlighted to the advantage of the island's name, but, in view of tradition as well as quality, I am inclined to single out Nykteri from Canava Roussos. One of the most fully yellow dry wines around, Nykteri's richness of colour is reflected most of all in the deep yellowishness it holds even at the outermost rim of the glass, with no tendency to brownishness. Only its lustre hinders perception of that richness. Matured for six to seven years in barrel, the 13° Nykteri has both a bouquet of honeyed fruit and a characteristic earthiness of smell, unique to Santorini, that seems to lie where garlickiness links up with smokiness. In the mouth, Nykteri is full-bodied, with ample fleshiness of texture to balance a kind of tactile edge not encountered in other dry white wines at its lofty level of quality. Many would mistake it for a red in closed-eyes tasting; it is not alone among Santorini's whites in that respect. Nykteri should be considered especially as an accompaniment to smoked fowl, roast kid and *cassoulet*, and goes well with garlicky dishes generally. Nor do ripe Fontina, Brie and blue-veined cheeses overwhelm Nykteri.

Something must also be said of the disinherited Santorini wines, the reds, which are not entitled to an appellation of origin. When the appellation regulations for Santorini were drawn up in 1971, Greek enological authorities regarded incentives for increased planting of the black *mandilariá* as undesirable, because it might occur at the expense of the *asýrtiko*, which is considered more typical of Santorini, and generally more crucial to wine quality there. Also, some Greek wine professionals sought to keep red wine out of the island's entitlement because of a negative bias rooted in the circumstance that during most of this century island red wines have mostly been *broúsko*s literally made to order for blending. Based on that commercial necessity, it became an almost axiomatic belief among some non-Santoriniote Greek wine specialists that nothing of high quality could be expected of Santorini in the way of dry *mandilariá* wine. Yet back in the days before Santorini was reduced to a source of blending-wine, Western travellers in the Aegean knew the island to have the capability of yielding excellent dry red. For instance James Denman, who seems to have been the only nineteenth-century wine writer ever to visit Santorini, testified to it in one of the more puzzling wine descriptions on record: 'The best red growth is called Santorin, and being dry, spirituous, and agreeable to the palate, a rich Claret in character with a genuine Port-wine flavour, well sustains the high reputation it has acquired' (*The Vine and its Fruit*, 1864). But anyone who tries to describe Santorini's wines tersely can sympathize with Denman's predicament.

Markezinis and Roussos have been experimenting with dry red wine with a view to producing outstanding products at a level of alcohol content below the traditional range. Markezinis's Santinos red is a *mandilariá* wine of 12.2° alcohol, matured for four to five years in oak, while the Cava Atlantis red that he plans will have more age at bottling, and more alcohol. Roussos has concentrated his efforts on Caldera, a 13.5° *mandilariá* wine aged for six to seven years in barrel. Santinos and Caldera are dark ruby in colour, certainly among the darkest wines bottled in the Aegean. The medium-bodied Santinos is the easier to drink at the time of bottling, although it has repaid several years' keeping. Caldera is full-bodied, with a notable astringency which some will find distracting until the wine has at least several years of bottle-age. At any age, however, to serve Caldera at all chilled is liable to prove a disappointing experience. On Santorini, try Santinos red or Caldera with a plate of the island's fava beans, to enjoy the flavours of Santorini in all their glory, or else with the stuffed eggplant dish *papoutsákia* (slippers).

Canava Roussos is the only island winery to have bottled *visánto* wines recently. A rosé version has particularly impressed me. It is obtained from *mandilariá* with admixture of *asýrtiko* and *aïdáni áspro*. Fermentation takes place with stalks and stems, and bottling comes about a decade later. Like all *visánto*, Canava Roussos's rosé is so sweet that most people can only take it in small doses, and even then only by intermittent sipping. It tries the patience and thirsty gullet of some ('some people feel most impelled towards wine when the drink they most want is water', Plutarch, *Moralia*, 'Table-talk'). A few perhaps will find it impossible to take to the sweetness at all. The Englishman Bent called *visánto* 'abominably luscious', and even the Santoriniote Markezinis disparagingly calls it 'a syrup'. One should, however, try the wine at various ages before making such inflexible judgments.

Canava Roussos Visanto rosé at first baffles the taster who expects familiar rosy shades, and never so much as when newly bottled, for then it presents a brownish-orange hue approaching reddishness, while also working towards a golden-green at the rim. It is a most finely structured progression of tints. Aromas associated with those of dried stone fruits like apricots and prunes are plainly in evidence; in suggesting a comparability between *visánto* and Commandaria, Edmond About described the latter as becoming brown with age, and resembling prune juice in flavour as well as colour ('amateurs often pay very dear for putting into their cellars, that which they might have for nothing from their kitchens'). But there is much more to Visanto's bouquet than the browning of fruit sugars. Like so many Santorini wines, it displays distinctive 'earthy' smells which have no remote approximation in the wines of other places. In due course, a bitterish tone also appears, together with the aftermath of acidity fostering a sensation reminiscent of limes.

Perhaps the most amazing thing about Visanto is that it has an alcohol content of only 8.5°. It is nevertheless unassailably, consummately, vinous. Elsewhere in the wine world, the particular phenomenon of low alcohol and imposing vinosity has been recorded only at Tokaj, and there only in the case of genuine *essencia*, a wine (or syrup?) which would only be sold for a king's ransom. Yet Canava Roussos Visanto can be purchased for next to nothing, or scarcely more drachmas than one would pay for a bowlful of limes, prunes and dried apricots. It goes on in bottle indefinitely, too, albeit mellowing as it goes, which will not, I suspect, be preferred by everyone. A considerable sediment is thrown even if Visanto is kept only several years, so that it usually needs decanting, and preferably two or three days ahead of time if older than fifteen years or so altogether. Enjoy a glass with an unpeeled peach, or a slice of that rather liquid American confection from pecans, which tenuously slips by under the rubric 'pie'.

CLASSICAL REFLECTIONS

Among the written works remaining from antiquity there is none corresponding to a modern popular book on wine, and the information about wine that is available to us in the ancient record usually is not presented in a way that relates the nature of specific wines to particular wine-making techniques. The result is that it is most difficult to compare a specific wine of modern Greece to one of the ancient era without over-indulging in speculation about ancient wine and falling into the trap of self-delusion. However, there is an exception, and it pertains to *visánto*.

Drying grapes in the sun has been employed virtually throughout the Aegean since antiquity. The drying takes place on a specially suitable surface called a *liástra*, or 'sunner', which is the *iliastírion* of antiquity; the wines which result from the vinification of those grapes are then called *liastó* (sunned). Usually the *liástra* is a particularly suitable spot among the vineyards and fields. On Santorini, however, although the latter sort of *liástra* is not unknown, the typical kind used in making *visánto* has been the flat rooftops of the traditional cellars. Moreover, the rooftop position of the grapes is protected by a low wall built all around the perimeter of the roof. Alternatively, the grapes for *visánto* are 'baked' in enclosed courtyards by the cellars. In view of all this, but especially of the placing of grapes in a raised position, it is nearly impossible not to recall the ancient Greek wine called *diákhyton*, mentioned by the Roman Pliny:

> a wine called in Greek 'strained wine' ['diachyton' (*sic*)], to make which the grapes are dried in the sun for seven days raised seven feet from the ground on hurdles, in an enclosed place where at night they are protected from the damp; on the eighth day they are trodden out, and this process produces a wine of extremely good bouquet and flavour.
>
> (*Natural History*)

Yet what is most relevant to *visánto* in Pliny's mention of *diákhyton* is that he identified that wine as belonging to the class of wines falling 'between the sirops and real wines'. Also included in that class were *aigleucos*, or 'Ever-must', *prótropon*, or 'First-urged' (the wine produced from the juice expressed by the weight of the grapes themselves), and wine produced from honey and must. The wines concerned would have been distinguished not only by their relatively high sugar content, but also by their relatively low alcohol content, which would have been occasioned by the very great concentration of sugar in the indicated musts, and a consequent greatly burdened fermentation. And then, too, 'real wines' for Pliny were those of relatively high alcohol content, an exemplar being Maronean, which he noted was drunk with twenty parts water in Homer's time, in order to temper the alcohol. In this regard it must be noted as well that Aegean *liastó* wines, including ones so called on Santorini, are of 15–16° alcohol, rather than the 8–9° of *visánto*.

Visánto is probably the sort of Greek wine most likely to engender musing about ancient wines on account of its own features, rather than just one's own propensity to do so. For as it ages, *visánto*'s tremendous vigour subsides, so that the taster becomes most conscious of its viscosity, and in that way is reminded of wines the ancient writers mentioned as 'sweet' and 'thick'. Indeed, a twenty-year-old bottle of Canava Roussos Visanto might be decanted, with a bit of it then being left in the decanter for two weeks or so, at which point it bears an equal volume of water in such a way as pleasurably to recall Aristotle's statement that 'well-mixed wine obscures all perception of water, and only gives a sensation of soft wine' (*Problems*).

One school of thought has it that the ancients doted on wines so thick as to demand mixture with water if they were to be drunk, rather than ingested as an early form of Greek 'spoon sweets'. Pliny is often cited in that regard, since he mentioned 200-year-old wines which had been 'reduced to the consistency of honey' (*Natural History*). But it is just as frequently overlooked that he also went on to say that those wines were unpleasant to drink even if well watered, and instead were reserved 'as a seasoning for improving other wines'. It is Aristotle, however, who really sets the record straight, by mentioning wine among the 'watery liquids' which are 'affected by drying [evaporation]' (*Meteorologica*). Elsewhere he even cast aspersions on the winehood of sweet wines, so that it must be doubted whether they were of such great popularity as has often been assumed by historians of wine:

> Why do not men become drunk under the influence of sweet wine, which is more pleasant? Is it because sweet wine has a flavour which does not belong to wine, but to something else? The man who is under its influence [that is, has become drunk on it] is therefore rather fond of the sweet than fond of wine.
>
> (*Problems*)

Aristotle may have identified that 'something else' as excessive 'oiliness', since in *Meteorologica* he notes that oil 'gives off fumes but does not evaporate'.

In considering the ancients' attitude towards the sweetest wines, it is useful to refer to Hippocrates. He explained that what is uncompounded in taste is 'strong', since it is undiluted and unopposed, and by definition necessarily 'painful', because it works on the palate rather in the way of a primal force:

The strongest part of the sweet is the sweetest, of the bitter the most bitter, of the acid the most acid, and each of all the component parts of man has its extremes . . . for there is in man salt and bitter, sweet and acid, astringent and insipid, and a vast number of other things, possessing properties of all sorts, both in number and in strength. These, when mixed and compounded with one another are neither apparent nor do they hurt a man; but when one of them is separated off, and stands alone, then it is apparent and hurts a man.

(*Ancient Medicine*)

To avoid the pain of unmitigated sweetness in wine, resort was often made to the use of flavouring substances; Theophrastus noted that sweet wine, 'because it has no "relish" of its own', is especially in need of the savouriness of a well-chosen additive (*Concerning Odours*), much as we might 'spike' stewed plums with mace. Hence the appreciation that would have been felt for any sweet wine with sufficient 'relish' of its own:

the mixed [savour] is pleasanter than the unmixed, if one can achieve perception of both elements at the same time. For wine is pleasanter than oxymel because things mixed by nature are more completely blended than when mixed by us. For wine is a mixture of bitter and sweet flavour. The so-called wine-pomegranates prove this.

(Aristotle, *Problems*)

But even more to the point, so does Santorini's *visánto*.

5

Paros and the Cyclades

There can be no doubt whatsoever that Paroikia is built on the ruins of the ancient Pariote capital . . . there is a church dedicated to the Drunken St George. Here, I thought, must be a true descendant of Bacchus; an instance of how the Greeks still love to deify their coarser passions; and on enquiry I was told that on November 3, the day of the anniversary of St George's death, the Pariotes usually tap their new-made wine and get drunk . . .
(James Bent, British traveller, *The Cyclades*, 1885)

Sometimes it may seem as though no stretch of Winedom has been left uncharted, and that no true adventures are left for the wine traveller. All the more reason to approach the Cyclades and happily prove oneself wrong: these islands are almost always left off wine maps today. Named for the circle (*kýklos*) they seemed to form around the holy island of Delos during antiquity, they comprise around twenty significant islands that spread south-eastward in rather angularly arranged clusters from off the seaward tip of Attica, which is Sounion, into the mid-southern Aegean, beginning with Tzia (Kea) and ending with Amorgos.

There is no little irony in the obscurity of the Cyclades at this late date, since it was an area to which Dionysus formed a particular attachment at a very early time. Cycladic wine exports were so considerable during antiquity that the first-century BC Roman agriculturist Columella, in his *De Re Rustica*, indicated them as a reason for Latium's preference to import wine rather than cultivate the vine in his day. The productivity of the Cyclades continued through Byzantine times, and into recent centuries as well. Cycladic wines also went westward in modern times, although few Westerners who drank them were aware of their origin, since the Cyclades were an important source of malvasia, a wine usually sold only under its

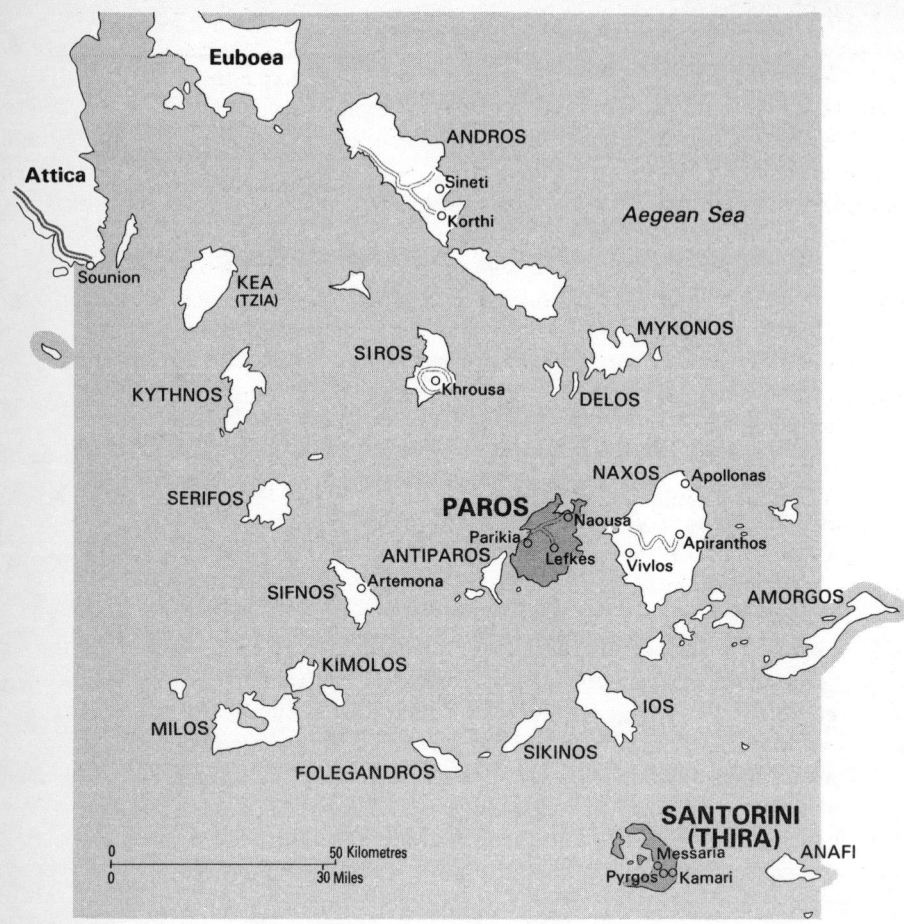

The Cyclades

generic name. In the nineteenth century, however, the Cyclades drifted ever further towards the periphery of the European economy, becoming increasingly dependent on the West and constrained to export what was asked of them. After phylloxera struck France, what was asked of the Cyclades was blending-wine. In the twentieth century, distantly headquartered Greek wine companies, no more concerned than their Western counterparts about encouraging the best efforts, joined in patronizing the Cyclades.

PAROS

While the legacy of blending-wine production still hangs over the traditions and name of the Cyclades, a breach has been made in its formidable walls. This has been achieved at Paros, a largish member of the group that lies far closer to its geographical centre than does Delos. Paros was a prestigious producer of malvasia, but none the less, or perhaps all the more, targeted by the blending-wine buyers. In recent decades, sales of blending-wine for the making of generic Greek rosé wines for export westward have been the mainstay of Pariote viticulture. The island could hardly have looked forward to any other role in wine, until improved Greek economic conditions in the 1970s, and perhaps most of all the influence of tourism, opened up other possibilities. The bottling of wine was undertaken, and in 1981, contrary to what anyone expected of Paros a decade earlier when Greece had provided for the granting of appellations of origin, the island was elevated to appellation of origin status on the basis of a type of dry red wine which combines the best of island traditions with technologically sound, contemporary enological practice. It is indeed cause for Bacchic revelry in the Cyclades.

Weather conditions on Paros more or less typify those which influence Cycladic wine-growing generally. Although characterized by an absence of rain during the growing season, the Pariote climate is somewhat humid, but variably so from year to year, so that annual conditions for grape maturation vary as well. Air currents do not have the profound impact that they have on Santorini, but breezes can be stiff, and have influenced traditional vine cultivation techniques. Apparently in order to protect young shoots from the breezes, the stocks of the vines are typically encouraged to grow at a sharp incline, so that the tendrils will creep along the ground. Such tendrils, called *aplotariés* (spreaders, but perhaps more accurately described as runners), can reach up to 5 metres or so in length. Consequently grape clusters, too, grow by the ground in such instances ('All the vines about Lesbos, being neither high-grown nor propped with trees, incline themselves and protend their palmits towards the ground, and creep like the ivy; so that indeed a very infant, if that his hands be loose from his swathes, may easily reach and pull a bunch,' Longus, *Daphnis and Chloe*, second to third century AD).

Varietal make-up on Paros is also very typical of the Cyclades, all of the varieties grown being usual ones for this part of the Aegean.

The blending-wine trade appears to have had a serious negative impact on Paros's varietal profile, however, in that it favoured the unbridled spread of the tannin-rich black *mandilariá*, a variety not entirely well suited to the island. Judging by the *mandilariá*'s predominance even in old vineyards in the upland interior of Paros, it may be supposed that it has long been the major variety. Still, without a crucial commercial role it is unlikely that the *mandilariá* would have achieved the 85 per cent hold on island vineyard area that it had in the years prior to the Second World War. Because it is a relatively late-ripening variety, in this case planted in an environment where a humid summer can delay ripening and cause rotting, the *mandilariá*'s performance is markedly variable from one year to the next at all island sites, irrespective of their exposure, elevation and soil composition. It was perhaps in empirical recognition of the idiosyncratic behaviour of the *mandilariá* on their island that traditional Pariote wine-makers attentive to quality have taken care to limit its role in their wines, especially dry red ones. Its usefulness for blending enabled the *mandilariá* to gain ground none the less, and also stimulated planting of it on low-lying, poorly drained soils, unsuitable for the production of quality dry red wine in any year.

While the *mandilariá* was extending its territory, Paros's chief white variety, the *monemvasiá* (usually called *monovasiá* by growers), was in decline. The variety's name, which is that of the place on the Peloponnesian coast to the west where malvasia was once made, suggests an arrival on the island in the late Middle Ages, when the malvasia trade began to grow in importance. For malvasia production, grapes high in sugar content were needed, and the *monemvasiá* suited the purpose ideally, being an early-ripening sort that continues to increase in sugar content for virtually as long into the Pariote growing season as it is allowed to remain on the vine. When grown at relatively higher elevations on the island, and cultivated well, the *monemvasiá* is capable of yielding high-quality wine of a sweet and alcoholic nature, yet not lacking in acidity. The loss of the malvasia trade and the later uptake in the blending-wine trade, however, caused both a loss in plantings and less careful tending of the *monemvasiá*. Finally, without a real economic role the variety lost still more ground in the post-war period, when the higher yielding *savatianó* was brought from the mainland.

The historical circumstances of island viticulture encouraged an assortment of habits among island wine-makers. Some of the most popular are unacceptable from the standpoint of contemporary, world-standard wine-making. Notably, the practice of letting the *monemvasiá* gain as much sugar as possible during maturation, in order to increase alcohol content in the wines, and thus disease-resistance as well, results in wines both overly alcoholic and deficient in acidity for cosmopolitan tastes today. Also, to obtain drier-tasting white wines from those grapes, some Pariotes started adding water to the must, which has the effect of reducing acidity along with sugar content. Some islanders, however, have made wines from a mix of red and white grapes, a practice also encountered elsewhere in the Cyclades. When the wines are made skilfully from properly ripe grapes, the results can be very admirable. The Greek Wine Institute, in considering the awarding of an appellation of origin to Paros, therefore chose that strain of Cycladic tradition. Consequently the appellation regulations for Paros call for a dry red wine produced from a must that is two-thirds *monemvasiá* and one-third *mandilariá*, with the proportion having to be measured in terms of grape weight, since *mandilariá* grapes and *monemvasiá* must are combined in the vat for vinification. Until 1989, however, a proportion of half and half was permitted in order to allow time to extend plantings of the *monemvasiá*.

The Wine Institute's main partner in developing the appellation requirements was the Union of Agricultural Cooperatives of Paros, with its headquarters at the chief island town and port of Parikia. The Union produces 25,000–30,000 hectolitres of wine annually, from various parts of the island. Nearly two-fifths of the must comes from the western coast, in the vicinity of Parikia, while another fifth comes from the Naousa area on the north-eastern coast. Both areas are predominantly low-lying, at less than 20 metres above sea level. By common consent of the Pariotes, the best wine grapes come from the mid-island village of Lefkes, whose steeply inclined, north-east-facing vineyards are the highest on Paros, at 300–400 metres. But Lefkes is a relatively small producer, and the Union purchases only about 5 per cent of its grapes there. Additionally, about one-tenth of the Union's must originates on Antiparos, Paros's sister island just off its south-western coast; Antiparos is not included in the appellation Paros zone. Growing only red wine varieties, Antiparos produces some of the best *mandilariá* grapes, which probably explains the nineteenth-century visitor Bent's having tasted an 'excellent wine' there, but also the variety called *váftra* (or *vápsa* (tinter) for its coloured pulp. The *váftra* gained ground in the late nineteenth century, when Bent noted Antipariote wine being 'sent to France to make claret with', an instance of the sort of 'incentive' that has particularly contributed towards keeping the Cyclades 'down on the farm' in the twentieth-century world of wine.

The Union has mostly produced, and continues to depend on, wine for blending. Furthermore, in so far as it has bottled, it has been constrained by financial considerations to concentrate on sound wines of average quality, especially the trio of its Trovatore series: a white (*monemvasiá*), a rosé (*mandilariá*) and a red (*mandilariá* with a little *váftra*), all at 12° alcohol. Only the medium-bodied Trovatore white would be likely to attract a second look from abroad. More recently a red called Madon has appeared, intended as a step up from Trovatore red. A Retsina from *savatianó* is also produced, as well as a dry white called Nisiotissa, which is made from lesser *monemvasiá* grapes from some of the better vineyards of the semi-mountainous area. Nisiotissa is the Union's vain attempt at crispness, for which a price I deem too high is extracted from the wine: the absence of the discernibly Pariote character that requires no self-justification.

The wines produced and bottled by Manolis Moraïtis, who operates his winery at Naousa, bottling nearly 4,000 hectolitres annually, have generally been more attractive than the Union's wines. Over two-thirds of Moraïtis's wine is the product of his own vineyards and those of a number of other growers around Paros from whom he buys grapes. The rest is must bought from the Union. Moraïtis's better red and white wines are under the Kavarnis label, at 12° alcohol. Lagari is the label for his second-line pair, at 11.5°. Kavarnis white is made in about equal proportion from *monemvasiá* and *savatianó*, a very usual mix for home-made whites on Paros these days. Like Trovatore white, Kavarnis white has the acidity and aromatic flavour to place it among the 'fresh and fruity' white wines of Greece, although unfortunately it is not crisp. In favour of Moraïtis's medium-bodied Kavarnis red, I would say it is very good red wine by any standard, and was the best bottled red of Paros . . . until the Union came out with its appellation wine.

The Union made the island's first appellation wine, Paros, from the 1981 vintage, in accordance with the dispensation pertaining to the proportion of *mandilariá* and *monemvasiá*. The wine was marketed by the Botrys firm of Attica, with due attribution to the Union on the label. Paros is a 12° wine that is bottled after spending about fifteen months in barrel. The Union expects to turn out about 5,000 hectolitres of appellation wine annually in coming years, after adding the storage space needed to give that much wine its required year of maturation in oak. The addition is currently being implemented, in part with funds channelled from the European Community. Production of 8,000–10,000 hectolitres is hoped for in the more distant future, but that could well prove over optimistic. For one thing, the Union is liable to have competition in producing appellation wines. Moraïtis says that he will produce an appellation wine, and the Macedonian firm of Boutari has already produced and marketed a small amount of appellation Paros wine, a 12.5° wine under their Paros label, on a trial basis.

A more basic constraint on the production of appellation wine on Paros is the need for a very extensive replanting with *monemvasiá*. At present, the ratio of output between *mandilariá* and *monemvasiá* is approximately 3:1, which is rather the reverse of what the appellation requirement calls for. It is hoped that an increase in price offered for *monemvasiá* grapes will stimulate plantings, and certainly the competition of three major bottlers should help in that direction. The administrative step of halting plantings of *savatianó* has also been taken so as to benefit the *monemvasiá*. At present, over 800 hectares of vineyards are cultivated, but there is most definitely room for more, notably on the 200-metre-high ridge to the rear of Parikia. The island has not suffered phylloxera's ravages, but the ridge's extensive vineyards were devastated by a fire a couple decades back, and tourism, which tends always to be a double-edged knife for Greek wine, has in the meantime assumed such significance in the Pariote economy that viticulture must take a back seat to the service industry. However, another factor hindering optimal output of the appellation wine is the difficulty in finding suitably ripened grapes of both the *mandilariá* and *monemvasiá* varieties to be harvested the same day, a practice found to produce the best wine for the contemporary world market.

One might not expect a wine with the varietal make-up of appellation Paros red to be *really* red. Nevertheless, the Union's Paros is indeed a most dark red, despite the removal of the *mandilariá* skins after only two days of fermentation. It ought to be emphasized, however, that it is a definitive *red*ness, just short of that truly violet cast which generally qualifies Pariote red wines as 'black' in the islanders' eyes, although it could be said that Paros offers a colour quite like the darkest flesh of 'black' cherries exposed by a bite. Aromatically, the newly bottled wine displays several facets: berry fruits, sweet spices and balsamic smells, all in their sweetest manifestation. Perhaps the strongest tug is in the direction of sweet spices, which seems to be the case with Pariote red wine generally. Several years of bottle age weave the several aromatic threads more closely, but the wine is eminently drinkable right at bottling, even by people without much taste for tannic red wine, and that is perhaps the best time at which to experience and enjoy the very characteristic feel of Pariote wine. Paros is soft initially, because of texture, and remains unobtrusive on the sides of the tongue throughout the duration of a mouthful. Yet, it is not at all flabby. Does it have anything to do with island morphology? Bent wrote that Paros, which enjoyed singular fame for its marble during antiquity, 'is nothing but one huge block of marble covered with a thin coating of soil' – a not entirely accurate depiction – and Pliny mentioned that the ancient Greeks sometimes added marble dust to wine to make it softer. But at rock bottom, the influence of the Pariote bedrock on the island wines is a mystery to me.

If the elegance of marble does not rub off on Pariote wine, Paros none the less is quality dry red wine that would not disgrace tables with more elegant veneers than formica. Some people might find in it the advantage of a chameleon-like quality as an accompaniment to food: its property of varied flavour sensations, so evenly arranged within the whole, that the wine remains recognizably itself even as one detects the equilibrium of sensations shifting this way or that under influence of the food. I have therefore been unable to persuade myself that some intrinsic quality might cause beef, lamb, pork, or even chicken to be the preferred meat with Paros, although, perhaps overlooking that even marble can be ground to a fine dust, my reckoning is that newcomers to the wine will spot its merits the better with certain ground meat dishes, such as *soudzoukákia*, which are minced meat rolls flavoured with cumin and served with a special tomato sauce. I will cautiously mention meatloaf too, hoping not to disparage Paros by doing so. I might really sabotage its prospects for respect by recommending, with a view to side dishes for meatloaf and such, that here at last is a red wine suited to everything about the essence of beets. Less controversially, I would suggest a variety of cheeses, especially semi-soft ones. Havarti, Edam, Gouda and Munster perhaps have an advantage when flavoured with caraway, cumin or cloves. Mild varieties of the Cheddar family nevertheless seem as good, and one need not carry home bottles to check on it. I have no idea what cows are doing in the Cyclades, but at Prodromos, on the eastern side of Paros, the cooperative dairy uses local cows' milk to produce a very good, semi-hard cheese distinctly reminiscent of Cheddar types. The differences of kind can be attributed to the influence of marble on the cow's forage.

In the future the Pariotes would like to see an extension of their appellation entitlement. It is believed that Pariote dry white wine can be deserving, but given the present shortage of *monemvasiá*, a move in this direction would spell decreased production of the more typical red. Furthermore, in order to meet contemporary tastes a new method of vine cultivation, most likely entailing a system of high-trained vines, might have to be inaugurated at least in some areas of the island. On another front, the Union is hopeful of gaining Paros an appellation for semi-sweet red wine from sun-dried grapes, a type of wine in which Paros is deemed to have advantages. In Lefkes, where it is averred that the best is produced, up to fifteen or sixteen varieties of grape, most of which are planted to only a very minor extent, are used for it, but always with *mandilariá* dominant. After spending about one week in the sun, the grapes are crushed and the must fermented with the stems as well as the skins. The wine is sometimes made and kept in chestnut, in order, it is said, to obtain the preferred darker colour. The 16° semi-sweet wine is popular in part because of the feeling of warmth it engenders in the cold weather, when most of it is drunk, beginning in November as Bent mentioned back in 1885.

THE CYCLADES

The wine explorer setting out to tramp the Cycladic donkey lanes and goat paths leading to such vinous treasures as remain could benefit from some advice, since it is all too easy to miss what one should be looking for, or else to mistake what one has found. Most of the Cyclades have not been touched by phylloxera, and the vineyards that have survived emigration, which has been an implacable foe of viticulture in this century, still reflect the complex varietal history of the islands. As a gross generalization about the Cyclades, it may be said that the varieties *mandilariá, monemvasiá, athíri* and *aïdáni áspro*, the last three of which reflect past involvement with malvasia production, are widespread, and tend to be more or less significant where they are found. However, Greek ampelographers have identified over sixty-five varieties in the Cyclades to date, and others besides the aforementioned ones can be quite important locally. The varietal confusion is not helped by the fact that the vineyards are planted with a multiplicity of varieties, but substantial conformity to a pattern is discernible at individual sites.

Two circumstances can throw wine buffs off the scent of local tradition. First of all, it is possible to run across anomalous wines, that is, ones whose occurrence is exceptional and the result of special circumstances. This would have happened to me at Lefkes on Paros had I not known beforehand that I was looking for semi-sweet red wines. I met a fellow who was producing a superb semi-sweet white wine in the malvasia tradition, the explanation for which turned out to be that he was a native of Naxos who had married into Lefkes and planted the vineyard his wife brought as part of her dowry with white varieties, so as to produce the sort of wine he had known on his native island. It is also possible to encounter one kind of wine virtually everywhere on an island and assume that it is *the* island wine, when in fact another kind from a particular village is traditionally the most esteemed wine, though so little is now made that nothing is heard of it by visitors. This can happen notably with retsina. Although resinated white wine is found virtually everywhere in the Cyclades today, possibly even to the exclusion of other wines in some places, it is not truly traditional. Bent came upon retsina only on Kythnos among the Cyclades in the late nineteenth century, and an elderly wine-grower on Paros told me that production there does not go back more than forty years or so. Retsina seems to have spread along with the *savatianó*, the usual mainland variety for this wine, since the Second World War.

A selection of Cycladic ports of call could usefully begin with Mykonos, which is as much the hub of the Cyclades for hedonists today as Delos was anciently for the religious. The stories tourists usually swap about the place are of interest to a wine traveller in so far as they reveal bareness as being as characteristic of Mykonos now as in antiquity, when Strabo noted the great frequency of baldness among the inhabitants. The islanders perhaps were already guilty anciently of crimes against Dionysus for which divine retribution was brought down on their heads. Anyhow, Tournefort alleged that what was sold as wine on Mykonos was 'mostly coloured water', while a century later Galt wrote that although there was a celebrated dry red resembling Bordeaux to be had, its producers 'will rather cheat you than give it genuine'. It might be unfair to consider such practices peculiar to Mykonos, and indeed Tournefort used his experience there to support his contention that the Greeks at large 'cannot forbear playing their tricks'. More recently, Philip Sherrard has considered that alleged Greek trait:

> Talented, versatile, indefatigably active, subtle, and insinuating, they prefer obtaining their object by intrigue and stratagem to gaining it honestly by industry and perseverance, in neither of which qualities, however, are they at all deficient.
>
> (*The Pursuit of Greece*, 1964)

We shall leave the Greeks to a perhaps uncharacteristic soul-searching, pondering the rewards of industry and perseverance in the new era that seems to be opening for them, but visitors to Mykonos are in the meantime advised to steer clear of bald wine-makers when looking for dry red wines based on the island's typical *ayianiótiko* variety!

Other islands of the northern Cyclades are Tinos, Andros and Syros. Tinos in the past was known for a variety of wines, including a malvasia made from *monemvasiá*, for which the island was famous. Today Tiniote wines are mostly dry, with semi-sweet ones made largely from the old variety *potamísia*, which takes both a black and a white form. Grapes intended for semi-sweet wine are dried in the sun for about a week and mixed with a little water during crushing. Andros, the northernmost and one of the largest of the Cyclades, did not have the reputation of its neighbours, but the early visitor Paul Lucas (1714) was not apprised of that and thought the island's wines 'exquisite'. He was particularly impressed to find them being matured in barrel for six years or so, which was unusual in Western Europe in those times, before bottles came into vogue and when such ageing as a wine received occurred in barrel. Ravaged by phylloxera, Andros has now been substantially replanted, and some of the red wines of the villages of Korthi and Sineti in the south are once again showing that Lucas was not exaggerating much on quality, bearing in mind that in those times tastes might have been more amenable to rather heady wine. Significant on Andros are the grape varieties *armeletoúsa*, *koumári* and *potamíssi* (*potamísia*), all black. To the south, Syros grows mainly black and white variants of the *xylomakheroúda* variety. Khrousa, south of the island port and capital of Ermoupolis, is the best-known wine area of Syros.

Among the southern Cyclades, large Naxos, which lies just east of Paros, stands out by reason of history. The island was considered sacred to Dionysus, and produced one of the earliest of the renowned Aegean vintages, Bibline: 'But at times let me have a shady rock and wine of Biblis . . .' (Hesiod, *Works and Days*, seventh century BC). Although there is a village called Vivlos in the central western part of the island, the name of the ancient wine is thought to have been taken from that of an island stream, probably in order to suggest free-flowing abundance. Naxos kept its repute for millennia, and was a producer of malvasia. The wine held in most special esteem even today is a sweet white one produced mostly from *aïdáni áspro* and *athíri*, at the high east-central village of Apiranthos. However, only a little of that wine is made now. Most Naxiote wine is red and from Apollonas, at the northernmost tip of the island, where a number of typical Cycladic red varieties are grown, such as *mandilariá, váftra, rodítis* and *mavrostáfylo*. The vineyards of Apollonas sit above marble that is second only to Pariote.

Off to the south-west from Naxos is sizeable Milos, which has certainly had its up and downs. In 1717, Tournefort called its wines 'exquisite' and said they were the equal of the best of Crete, for which his praise was unstinting. In 1788, however, Savary reported finding no native wine at all, owing to a loss of inhabitants to plague some years earlier. By the time Leake visited in the first half of the nineteenth century, some recovery had occurred, but wine quality was spotty. In the twentieth century, emigration has reduced availability. The *mandilariá* and the Cretan *liátiko* are the leading varieties grown for dry red wine on Milos. To the east of Milos, tiny Sikinos was known for its excellent sweet white wine produced from the *monemvasiá*, a little of which is still produced, despite the island's decimation by an emigration it could scarcely afford.

As with Mykonos in the north, I must single out Amorgos in the south and note a dubious distinction that was recorded in one of the old travelogues. The reporter in this case was none other than the Cycladist Bent, and his plaint was in having drunk wine from a goatskin that nearly made him become sick to his stomach. Bent's experience can be better imagined by considering Hobhouse's report from western Greece, in which he stated that 'the unpleasant strong savour of the goat in the new wine' was caused by the hairy side being turned inwards; furthermore, Theophrastus remarked that 'goat-skins are sympathetically affected when the breeding season comes round' (*Concerning Odours*). I am afraid that all of this puts Amorgos in a very bad light, and, as with Mykonos, not quite fairly. The facts are that wine-making practices representing various levels of technology manage to coexist happily in the Cyclades, and that the 'wine-skins' (*kraserá askiá*) have not entirely disappeared from any of the Cyclades, not even from recently upgraded Paros. On Amorgos, the wines to look for are red ones based on the old *voudómato* or *voïdomátis* (cow-eye) variety, and preferably in skin, to enable one to enjoy that archaic predecessor of today's prized and heady vinous perfume known as 'sweaty saddle'.

> On my shoulder in place of the wonted kirtle, bind, I pray, tight over my breast a dapple-back fawn-skin, full of the perfume of Maronian nectar, and let Homer and deep-sea Eidothea keep the rank skin of the seal for Menelaos. Give me the jocund tambours and the goatskins!
>
> (Nonnos, *Dionysiaca*)

CLASSICAL REFLECTIONS

The explorer Bent concentrated his life's work in the Cyclades because he anticipated a bountiful hunting ground on which to spot vestiges of ancient Greek life. With bacchanalia in mind, he was particularly struck by the uninhibited Pariote celebrations that marked their tapping of the new wine on 3 November, the day of 'Drunken St George' (*Áyios Yeóryios Methistí*). Besides the carousal on Paros, Bent noted that on Serifos local aficionados made the rounds of the island's cellars on St Minas's Day, 11 November. Activities like that on Serifos take place on Santorini and Crete, respectively on the days of St Abercius (22 October) and Drunken St George, with the purpose of trying the newly made wines to see if they 'are drinking'.

With the exception of the one at Serifos, these respective events come about six weeks after the local vintages, which suggests that they were fitted into the Christian liturgical calendar according to long-standing experience as to the suitability of the new wines for drinking:

> the particular district makes a considerable difference even as between places which are not far apart; thus the crops of Salamis are far earlier than those of the rest of Attica, and so in general are those places by the sea.
>
> (Theophrastus, *Enquiry into Plants*)

Also, the concentration of the events in late October and early November may well have grown out of the age-old Aegean cycle of agriculture, wherein the clearing of the new wines generally coincides with a lull in field-work; on Crete, the October–November period in between the sowing of winter crops and the harvesting of olives is colloquially known as *katharomoústia*, or 'must-clearing', that is, 'clearing of the new wines', and is regarded a convenient and appropriate time for weddings. Consequently, on Serifos, where Bent reported that the vintage began on 6 August and the new wine was considered 'fit to drink' after a month's fermentation, the festivities were put off until the slack days of November.

The classicist E. R. Dodds (1960) has expressed his opinion that spring was the exclusive 'right time for holy drunkenness', because in ancient Athens the 'Feast of Cups' was included in the rites called 'Anthesteria', which celebrated blossoming, as the name indicates, and was held in the period from late February to early March, which comprised the month of Anthesterion and which, in the Aegean, could bring out the first blossoms. Surely early worshippers, who identified Dionysus with the mysteries of regeneration that they saw in the yearly budding of vines, must have derived a kindred feeling of self-renewal in a wine-fuelled revel at springtime. However, in further support of his view, Dodds states that the wine of the previous vintage was only then drinkable, which must be an idea that he took from Plutarch: 'those who drink the new wine at the very earliest, do so in the month of Anthesterion, after the winter is gone' (*Moralia*, 'Table-talk').

Yet it must be remembered that virtually all the information that remains to us concerning bacchanalia relates only to Athenian and Attic customs. Furthermore, there is too little information concerning the Little, or Rural, Dionysia of the Attic peasants, which was held in autumn, for us to be able to say categorically that new wine was not sampled until spring. Some customs, particularly in the countryside, might have harked back to times long before thought was given to 'wine maturation', when wine supplies were routinely finished off between one vintage and the next ('Chloe . . . served [the vintagers] with drink of the old wine', Longus, *Daphnis and Chloe*). In those days wine might have been drunk fairly soon after fermentation ended, or perhaps even sooner:

> The wine spurted up in the grape-filled hollow, the rivulets were empurpled; pressed by the alternating tread the fruit bubbled out red juice with white foam. They scooped it up with oxhorns . . .
>
> (Nonnos, *Dionysiaca*)

It ought to be noted too, lest one should get the wrong idea about the Pariotes because of their annual wine bash, that Dodds has explained the origin of ritualized bacchanalia as a probable reaction to 'spontaneous attacks of mass hysteria', instances of which he cites in recent Western European history, that 'kept it within bounds, and gave it a relatively harmless outlet'. They were also a successful resolution of what Dodds calls our 'ambivalence' towards wine: 'To resist Dionysus is to repress the elemental in one's own nature; the punishment is the sudden collapse of the inward dykes when the elemental breaks through perforce and civilization vanishes.' Anyhow, the Pariotes have the reputation of being the most even-tempered and fair-minded of all Aegean inhabitants, so much so that Tournefort noted they were usually called in to arbitrate disputes among other Cycladic islands.

GASTRONOMIC NOTES

If Cycladic gastronomy can be said to have a centre, it must be Sifnos, to the west of Paros. It is somewhat curious that the distinction should fall on Sifnos, for it is among the smaller islands of the group, has no product peculiar to it, and none of its products are thought of as 'best'. Even the island's onions, which are so plentiful that in Bent's time the expression 'give a Sifniote an onion' was equivalent to 'taking coals to Newcastle', were deemed by Tournefort to be inferior to those of Serifos. What has gained Sifnos its reputation is its cooks. Georges Moussa, a Frenchman who resided on Paros for several years and wrote a book each on Paros and Sifnos, gave me his theory that the Sifniotes probably developed their culinary skills as mess cooks on ships. From there, apparently, they graduated to Constantinople, where Bent observed that most cooks were in fact Sifniotes. Yet perhaps they were preordained for that role before signing aboard Aegean vessels, since the Sifniotes have long been master potters, a trade which must have developed in tandem with cookery.

The most highly regarded native Sifniote dish, really not reproduceable elsewhere because of the utter Sifnioteness of every ingredient in the pot – and the pot too for that matter – and of course said to cook to perfection in the traditional native ovens on Sifnos, is baked fava beans. But the Sifniote talent is amply demonstrated in a variety of *plats du jour* available in the island's modest eateries; Georges could hardly stop praising a hole-in-the-wall *rôtisserie* in the village of Artemona. The Sifniote wine to expect with them nowadays – one must make do with it even in Artemona – is retsina, a fact which perhaps need not be too much lamented if it is native wine that is sought; Sifniote retsina can be quite good, and in my experience about the most characteristic to be had outside Central Greece and Euboea.

The Cyclades are brimming with little-known local specialities which the tourist generally will not encounter. Rudimentary local marketing habits often make them invisible to the casual visitor, and sometimes seasonal or overall availability is an obstacle to the outsider's acquaintance. Prominent among the happy exceptions, which is not to say that the visitor will never need to make inquiries, are the *louzés*, or air-cured pork sausages, of Mykonos, the partridges (*pérdika*) of Kythnos, the 'baby beef' (*moskhári*) of Tinos, the octopus (*khtapódi*) of Paros and Milos, the oysters (*strídia*) of Milos, the tomato paste and fava beans of Santorini, the Turkish delight (*loukoúmi*) of Syros, the honey-and-sesame *pastéli* of Ios and Kythnos, and the sugar-coated almonds (*kouféta*) of Anafi. Country cheeses abound on most of the Cyclades. Soft *myzíthra*, made from sheep's or goat's milk, is especially good, popular and widespread. Various local versions have their adherents, the islanders being well attuned and very partial to native flavours, but certainly a special mention could go to that produced from goat's milk at Pyrgos on Santorini. The excellent Santoriniote Easter cookie called *melitíni* requires soft *myzíthra*. A hard version of the cheese, called *xiro-myzíthra*, is also available.

Naxos is a special case: 'Everywhere huge piles of melons, peaches, and figs . . . drowsy Naxiot [*sic*] well-being' (Kazantzakis, *Report to Greco*). The ancients thought it was the most favoured of the Cyclades on account of the abundance and quality of its fruit, which perhaps is why they especially associated Dionysus with that island. Naxos is also said to yield the best olive oil of the Cyclades, and its large, green *throúmbes* table olives are well known. There is also outstanding *kefalotýri* cheese and Apiranthos ham (*zambón Apirán-thou*). The finishing touches to the soporific Naxiote table come with the island figs, whose quality caused the visiting Lord Charlemont (1749) to remark that 'Those of Marseilles, so greatly esteemed by us, are insipid when compared to them,' and the spirit called *kitrórako*, which the Naxiotes make from their citrons.

PART II
MAINLAND GREECE

6

Macedonia

The red wines of Macedonia of the areas of Naousa, Amyntaion, Ayios Panteleimonas, Goumenissa, Kozani, Grevena, Arnea, and others, present an excellent harmony of composition, analogous to certain choice red wines internationally recognized.
  G. Georgakopoulos, Greek enologist, *The Composition and Quality of the Wines of Macedonia*, 1957

Greece is not wholly an olive grove. That most characteristic Mediterranean fruit will not grow at all in some places. On the circuitous train ride to south-western Bulgaria from Thessaloniki, the chief city and port of the northern Greek region of Macedonia, the disappearance of olive trees is a readily observable change in scenery as the train heads inland, and they are soon replaced by a variety of deciduous fruit trees and generally rather northern vegetation. The shift is as indicative as anything might be of entering a part of Greece having an agricultural and gastronomic tradition divergent from Aegean patterns and particulars, a tradition which is apparent as well in wine.

In its inland and upland parts, Macedonia virtually duplicates the natural environment found across the borders, in the Pirin section of south-westernmost Bulgaria and below Skoplje in southernmost Yugoslavia. A sure sign of the similarity in traditional tastes is the graduated esteem in which *raki* is held going northward from Thessaloniki. A potent distilled beverage, *raki* can be found made from any of a number of fruits in northern Macedonia, and is much appreciated there during the rigorous winters. Indeed, ever since Greece acquired the region in 1913, agricultural experts concerned with reducing surplus national wine production, which is concentrated in the south, have regarded *raki* as a local competitor tending

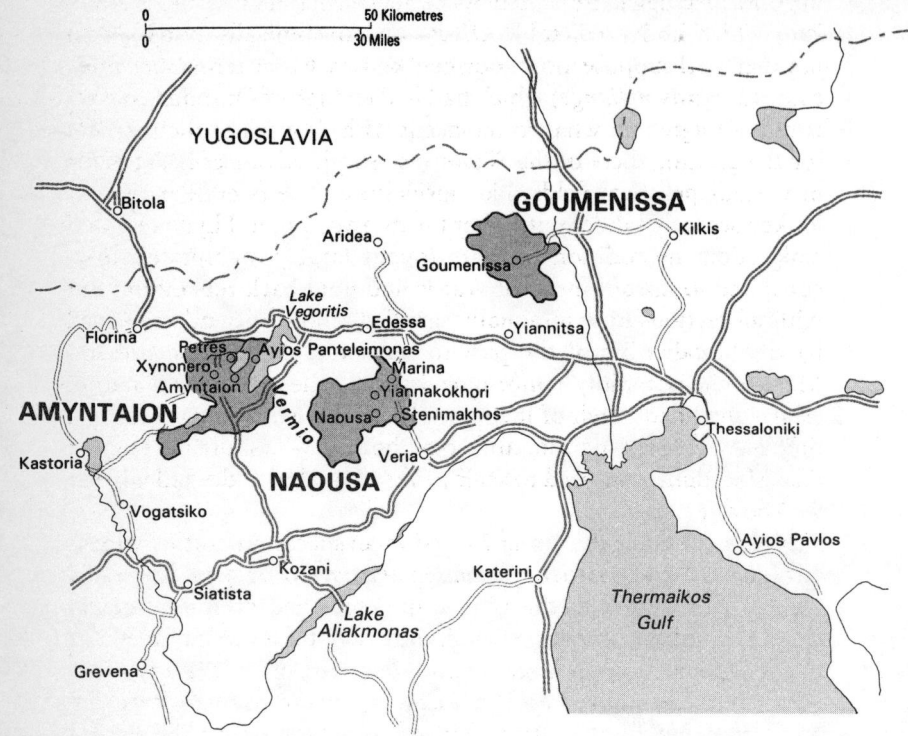

Western and Central Macedonia

to hold back wine consumption in rural Macedonia. Relatively low wine consumption in Macedonia has not, however, been a circumstance attributable only to a taste for *raki*. Historical factors have also been at play.

Numerous areas of Macedonia had vines during the centuries of Ottoman rule. The seventeenth-century Turkish traveller Evlia Chelebi ticked off a string of places across Macedonia having abundant vineyards: (moving from west to east) Kastoria, Skopia, Florina, Edessa, Naousa, Veria, Zikhni, Serres, Doxato. In the early nineteenth century, the French traveller Ami Boué also found flourishing vineyards. As the nineteenth century progressed, however, Macedonia became inhospitable to peaceful pursuits like wine-growing. The region spent most of the century eating up its energies

in political struggles fomented by the new secular religion of national-
ism, which had predictable effects on an ethnically hotch-potch
population (I suppose most gourmets know why the term *macédoine*
came to signify *mélange*) which had had enough of Ottoman rule yet
could not agree on what to replace it with. It was not the moment
for the grafting there of the Western scientific advances being made
in various practical fields, like agriculture. The twentieth century
looked scarcely kinder until after the midway point. Phylloxera and
emigration, in addition to wars fought largely on this territory,
conspired to uproot most vineyards and hold back replanting. But
with all factions now minimally satisfied, and sufficiently sickened
by the bloodletting of the past to see some good in the present,
Macedonia is rapidly confirming itself as the cornucopia nature
clearly intended much of it to be. The region is making up for lost
time in wine-growing too, and some bottled wines already suggest
that Macedonia is poised to scale peaks of quality in dry red wine as
we know it.

Making possible the recent Macedonian success in bottled wine is
a traditional grape variety of the region, the *xynómavro* (sour/acid
black). Well suited to the semi-continental and even continental
climatic conditions under which it is grown, the *xynómavro* enjoys
near hegemony over a larger continuous area than does any other
red wine grape in Greece. Its domain extends from the eastern rim
of the mountains of central Macedonia, westward to the Pindos
Mountains at the far end of the region, south to Thessaly, and north
to around the Yugoslav border. Within that area are a dozen or so
locales known in the past for their excellent wine. While some of
those places still support vineyards, few have really recovered from
phylloxera. Among the notable sites awaiting rejuvenation are Siatista, Vogatsiko, Kozani and Grevena. Until now, only three places
have been substantially restored to their former regional importance:
Naousa, Goumenissa and Amyntaion. They are showing the *xynómavro* to considerable advantage, and it is to be hoped that wider
acquaintance with these wines will redound to the benefit of Macedonian wine places that are still languishing.

NAOUSA

The dominant constellation of mountains in Macedonia is that known as Mount Vermio. On a bluff of its south-eastern edge, facing a distant and unseen Aegean, the town of Naousa looks out over extensive vineyards, as well as neat orchards of fruit trees. Naousa's name apparently derives from Niaousta, and in turn from Nea Avgousta, which was how the Romans' name for the place, Nova Augusta, came out in Greek. The place has been inhabited since antiquity, a fact which the early nineteenth-century French visitor Cousinéry, taken by 'its beautiful vineyards', attributed to its great suitability for the vine. After the Ottomans arrived, the townsmen managed to wrest a few privileges, including a relatively bearable tax burden and the absence of a Turkish garrison, so that Naousa was able to maintain its vineyards and actually increase its commerce in wine.

It paid the Naousans to bring ingenuity to bear. Since the town did not have convenient conditions for underground cellars, the Naousans set about putting the underground waters of Vermio to work for them. The houses of wine merchants were constructed above the underground currents to allow the ground-level cellars to benefit from the cooling effects of the water below. The choice sites were adjacent to the stream Arapitsa, which runs through what naturally became the most valuable real estate in town, where the most substantial of Naousa's old homes are to be seen today. Thanks to their cellars, the Naousans could confidently give a long maturation in barrel to their very tannic wine, then produced by a long fermentation on stalks as well as skins. The French traveller Pouqueville, writing in 1826, noted that Naousa's wine was rarely drunk before four to five years of age. It was, however, a worthwhile wait for Naousa's wine merchants:

> The wine of Naousa is in Macedonia what the wine of Burgundy is in France; it sells at double the other wines, even those of the most nearby countryside. It is transported to Salonika and Serres, where it is much consumed.
>
> (Cousinéry, *Voyage dans la Macédoine*, 1831)

The premium paid for Naousan wine in Cousinéry's day must have been in part a reflection of greatly reduced availability, since the early nineteenth century had been most disruptive for Naousan wine-growing. In 1804, the political rivalry of two Naousan leaders came to a head, resulting in much destruction to the environs, and subsequent heavy tribute paid from town resources by the winning side for outside military forces that had been brought in to ensure victory. Only a year later, the British traveller Leake visited, and noted that all considerable merchants had vacated Naousa, leaving it a much diminished place. Hardly was a recovery in progress when an even greater disaster took its toll. As news of Greek rebellion against the Ottomans began to pour in during 1821, the Naousans, spurred by a temerity fostered by their centuries of privileges, armed themselves and declared independence. An Ottoman army was dispatched to quell the Naousan uprising with the result that about 2,000 inhabitants perished, while at least as many more fled permanently. In addition, extensive damage was done to the town, its cellars and its lands. When Cousinéry was there in the latter part of the decade he found that what had been a little town before the insurrection was only a village in the years following it. Those years were not favourable for wine production, making it all the more curious that Cousinéry, who well knew the town's recent past, made no qualifying remarks when he assessed Naousan wine, apparently in the rating framework of André Jullien, in a rather modest way: 'considered as *vin d'ordinaire* . . . really the best of all Turkey'. It was rather as though Michelin had awarded a restaurant one-star status in perpetuity based upon its troubled performance around the time of D-Day.

It is easy to get the wrong idea from Cousinéry, and too few contemporary wine-lovers make the sort of intimate acquaintance with Naousa that would encourage challenging the old rating. Yet now is the time to be doing just that. An appellation of origin has been authorized since 1971 for dry red Naousan wine made exclusively from *xynómavro* grapes grown in designated vineyard areas of Naousa town, as well as the villages of Stenimakhos, Yiannakokhori, Marina, Lefkadia, Kopanos and Trilofos. Nearly 700 hectares of vines are planted in the appellation zone alone, mostly on clay-pyrite soils lying between 150 and 300 metres above sea level. Several private wineries and a cooperative one are producing Naousan red wines, and they follow the same general wine-making procedure. Following the vintage in late September, the must is fermented on skins alone – no stems as in olden times – for about fifteen days, then for one to two weeks more with the skins removed.

The wines range from about 12–13° in alcohol, with *káva*, or 'reserve', wines usually towards the upper end. Appellation wines must have a minimum of one year in barrel, but in practice they are given one and a half to two years. The *káva* wines spend two to three years longer in oak. All of the appellation wines have been vintage-dated, while some of the reserve wines have not. Because producers of reserve wines chose to name those wines in ways which convey extra quality, they were not allowed to market them as appellation Naousa wines until legislation in 1989 made it possible.

Pride of historic place at Naousa belongs to the large Boutari wine firm, which is the oldest bottler of Naousan wine, dating back to 1879; it is not, however, an uninterrupted history. Although based in Thessaloniki, Boutari's main winery is at Stenimakhos, below Naousa. Visitors to Macedonia desirous of appreciating something of the background of contemporary Macedonian wine could hardly do better than to look around Stenimakhos. The village is inhabited by Greek refugee families from near Plovdiv (Philippopolis) in south-central Bulgaria, where most were expert viticulturalists at the renowned wine town of Asenovgrad, formerly called Stenimakhos and Stanimaka. They have been a significant factor in Naousa's recovery. Especially to Boutari's credit is its having led in the replanting of vineyards at Naousa after a long lapse in interest following the arrival of phylloxera several years before the First World War. The firm has about 50 hectares of its own in Yiannako-khori, most of which were planted between 1970 and 1975. When planting there, Boutari abandoned the old method of unsupported vines, instead adopting the training of vines along cordons, which has become the exclusive practice in the Naousan vineyards. Boutari produces about 15,000 hectolitres of appellation Naousa wine annually, for which about one-quarter of the grapes is their own fruit, while the rest is bought in from numerous small wine-growers. The firm's *káva* wine is Grande Réserve Boutari, a vintage-dated wine of 12.5°, which since 1983 has been produced solely from Boutari's Yiannakokhori estate. Earlier, the grapes were not all from within the appellation zone, and the wine was at 12°.

In terms of quantity, Boutari has only two major competitors on the Greek market for Naousan wine. By far the largest and indeed now the largest producer of Naousan wines, is the GAOS 'Naousa' Cooperative, whose members cultivate 350–400 hectares of vines within the appellation zone, as well as other vineyards outside the zone. The Cooperative, which boasts the most up-to-date cooperative winery in Greece at the present time, is turning out from 15,000 to 17,000 hectolitres of appellation wine annually. Their first vintage was in 1984, from which the appellation wine was bottled in 1986. A 13° reserve wine from that vintage was kept in barrel for four years and marketed in 1988 under the Cava Vaeni label. The reserve would have been ineligible for the Naousa appellation whatever its name, because nearly one-fifth of it was from *cabernet sauvignon*, a variety not authorized under the appellation regulations but now being grown in the region to a minor extent. The Cooperative offers lesser red and rosé *xynómavro* wines under the Vaeni label; its white wine in that series is a blend of 60 per cent Rhodian wine with *xynómavro* vinified for white wine.

The other major producer of Naousan wine is the Tsantalis firm. Although headquartered at Ayios Pavlos on the Khalkidiki peninsula south-east of Thessaloniki, Tsantalis maintains a winery just below the town of Naousa, again underscoring the old interest in Naousan wine throughout Macedonia. Tsantalis has about 20 hectares of vineyards, dating back to 1972, planted in the low-lying, rolling Strandza area of Naousa, but buys in about four-fifths of the grapes used to produce nearly 10,000 hectolitres of appellation wine annually – or at least that is the amount it was producing before the Cooperative appeared on the scene. Tsantalis produces no reserve wine from the Naousan vintage.

Several family wineries operated by locals are also producing and bottling Naousan wines. The largest of them is that of the Kastaniotis family, who have about 15 hectares by Marina, in the northern part of the appellation zone, where they planted in the late 1970s. From those vineyards exclusively, they produce about 1,600 hectolitres of wine in each vintage. A reserve wine of 12.6° was bottled and marketed under the Kava Kastaniotis label in 1988, after seven years in cask. Another firm is that of the Khrisokhoou brothers. They produce about 1,000 hectolitres each year, mostly from the 10 hectares of their own vines in the gently sloping Rodakino area adjacent to Naousa town. A supplementary 20–30 per cent of the grapes used come from two or three other excellent vineyard properties nearby. The Khrisokhoou vineyards were planted from 1976 onwards, and their first vintage was 1979, which yielded an appellation wine. They have since added a reserve wine, Kava Khrisokhoou, produced from selected grapes of the same vineyards.

Still smaller producers are Markovitis and Melitzanis. Markovitis makes about 450 hectolitres in a vintage, all the grapes for which come from his 6 hectares of vines planted up in Pola Nera, north-west of Marina, an upland area of the appellation zone where ripening can be slightly retarded in some years. Although Markovitis's vines were planted in 1970, he did not process any of the fruit himself until over a decade later. His first bottling was in 1983, when the 1981 vintage appeared under the Pigasos label, with appellation of origin. Subsequently he has occasionally also used a Château Pigasos label, and when he did his wine was disqualified for the appellation, on the Ministry of Agriculture's principle that unverifiable superior quality is suggested. A reserve wine is in the offing, and Markovitis is also considering expanding production by buying in some carefully selected grapes. A fourth small-scale winery is that of the Melitzanis brothers, who produce about 150 hectolitres annually, very largely from their own 3.5 hectares of vineyards, planted in 1973 in the Gastra area of Naousa. The first bottling was in 1978. Their reserve wine is Kava Melitzanis, which is of 13° alcohol and aged five years in cask.

The marketing of the Naousan wines varies with the size of the wineries. The Boutari, Cooperative and Tsantalis wines are distributed widely in Greece, particularly the first two, which benefit from highly developed marketing networks. All of those have been exported as well. The smaller wineries mostly market regionally, especially Melitzanis, a large part of whose wines are sold from their own shop in Naousa, at Dimarkhias 8–1. Nearby is the shop of the Khrisokhoou brothers, at Dimarkhias 41, but much of their wine is also sold in Thessaloniki and the towns of central Macedonia. Kastaniotis sells mostly in Athens, Thessaloniki and Kavala, but has exported as well, especially to West Germany. Markovitis's wine goes to various retailers in Macedonia and Athens, but he limits the quantity sold to any one of them, with the exception of the Kava Zakharopoulos shops of Athens, with whom he has a special arrangement.

GOUMENISSA

Way up in *rakí* country, about 30 miles to the north-east of Naousa near the Yugoslav border, the town of Goumenissa acquired an appellation of origin for its red wine in 1981. Though it is no Naousa by reputation, Goumenissa's name in wine might have travelled further than it did were it not for a disadvantageous trading location. The town was in the unenviable position of being caught between the marketing spheres of two most outstanding wine towns of Ottoman Europe, Naousa to the south-west, and Melnik, a once largely Greek town now in the corner of Bulgaria, to the north-east. Goumenissa could hardly get due recognition from where it sat. The new marketing spheres created as a result of the redrawing of borders after the Balkan Wars of 1912–13 would perhaps have helped to acquaint more Greeks with Goumenissa's wine, but the ravages of phylloxera prevented taking advantage of the new marketing possibilities until after the Second World War.

From a viticultural point of view, nothing about Goumenissa's location has ever been particularly unfortunate. Its vineyards, presently occupying about 150 hectares in the appellation zone, are set out on the eastern inclines of the Païko Mountains, in the range of about 250 metres above sea level. The slopes are situated where the southern Macedonian upland descends to meet the valley of the Axios, which is the Vardar of southern Yugoslavia, a river that empties into the Aegean not far west of Thessaloniki. The influence of the Aegean is felt more strongly than at Naousa, although the vintage nevertheless takes place in late September. The greater warmth together with the lower calcium content in the soil constitute the environmental situation generally averred to make Goumenissa's wine somewhat softer than Naousan, and relatively more early-maturing as well. Also, however, the varietal composition of the vineyards at Goumenissa makes a contribution, since the *xynómavro* is not alone there. A variety called *negóska*, from the Slavic name for Naousa, which is Negush, is also cultivated; and although it may be closely related to the *xynómavro*, it has a tendency to develop more sugar during ripening. Appellation regulations call for a must of *xynómavro* and *negóska* in a ratio of 4:1. Traditionally, a small amount of another dark variety, *séfka*, which is the *shefka* of southern Bulgaria, was also part of the blend for many Goumenissan wines. The *séfka* is still found sporadically, and finds its way into some home-made wines, but is likely to disappear as a consequence of appellation regulations.

Currently, two appellation Goumenissa wines are produced, one by the Boutari firm, and the other by a local individual, Yeoryios

Aïdarinis. Using purchased grapes, Boutari turns out about 2,000–2,500 hectolitres annually, while Aïdarinis produces only about 200 hectolitres, for which about half of the grapes come from his own 3 hectares of vines. Aïdarinis's first bottling was in 1983. A major point of divergence in the production of the two wines is that the Boutari version is initially fermented for about fifteen days on skins alone, while the Aïdarinis wine spends about ten to twelve days on stalks as well as skins, which is the traditional method at Goumenissa. Both wines are at about 12° alcohol and spend about fifteen months in oak before bottling under their respective Goumenissa labels; appellation regulations specify a one-year minimum in oak. They are vintage-dated wines. Boutari's is available almost as widely as its Naousan wines, but it is necessary as yet to go to central Macedonia to find Aïdarinis's.

AMYNTAION

In heading westward from Goumenissa, vineyards are seen only occasionally. Formerly the area was settled overwhelmingly by a Turkish Moslem population whose presence effectively excluded wine-growing. Newer residents, mostly Greek refugee families from Turkey, who have replaced the Turks, have for the most part adopted the farming of crops and orchards as being more lucrative than grapes. Only around the large village of Amyntaion in the vicinity of Lake Vegoritis, on the far side of Mount Vermio from Naousa, do vineyards once again come into their own as a significant feature of the landscape. The area had been badly hit by phylloxera around the time of the Balkan Wars of 1912–13, and initially was slow in recovering, in part because the main market for its wine was traditionally northward, especially around Bitola (Monastiri), in land ceded to Yugoslavia as a result of the war. However, the area's old reputation for wine – the local folk claim the place has traded wine since antiquity – brought viticulture to the attention of refugee families settling in that area in the late 1920s and 1930s. Vineyards consequently grew in number and size until the development was set back by the Second World War and the Greek Civil War, the latter being particularly severe because of the proximity of Communist Yugoslavia.

Nearly 550 hectares of vines are planted at present in the area entitled, since 1971, to the Amyntaion appellation. According to the legal demarcation, fifteen villages besides the name-giving one belong to the appellation zone: Ayios Panteleimonas, Vegoras, Petres, Xynonero, Lakkia, Kleidi, Antigonos, Maniaki, Rodona, Aetos, Pedino, Fanos, Agrapidia, Anargyri and Variko. However, only the first four of these and Amyntaion are of significance at present, and Ayios Panteleimonas and Xynonero alone supply the great majority of the grapes, including about four-fifths of those processed by the region's only producer of appellation wines, the Union of Agricultural Cooperatives of Amyntaion. The only grape variety authorized for those wines is the *xynómavro*, which is generally called *popólka* in this area where Slavophone Greeks are still found. (Amyntaion itself was known as Sorovits/Surovichevo until the conclusion of the Balkan Wars, when it was renamed after Amyntas, the father of Philip of Macedon, who in turn sired Alexander the Great.)

Although Amyntaion is only 20 miles distant from Naousa as the crow flies, it lies on the far side of Vermio, blocked off from the influence of the Aegean. As one penetrates the region by car from Naousa, the elevation changes almost imperceptibly, and it comes as rather a surprise to learn that Amyntaion is around 650 metres above sea level, or about twice the altitude of the vineyards in the upper part of the appellation Naousa zone. These features of Amyntaion's setting cause the local climate to be entirely continental, though moderated somewhat by the influence of Lake Vegoritis, and set the vintage back to mid-October. Annual fluctuations in grape quantity and quality are as wide as those known at northerly European red wine sites, and the climatic situation is further compounded by significant divergences in vineyard position and soil, especially between Ayios Panteleimonas and Xynonero. The former village is on the plains area just west of little Lake Petron, while the latter is on the slopes west of Amyntaion proper. Soil tends to be a sandy clay around Xynonero, and a sandy loam around Ayios Panteleimonas, with considerable variation in calcium content from vineyard to vineyard at both places. It is exactly the sort of environmental situation that led to the emphasis on vintage dates and individual vineyard properties which became characteristic of parts of Western Europe once economic conditions were ripe for it.

In surveying the varied conditions and wines of the region, viti-vinicultural researchers working at Amyntaion found a steady relationship in annual grape maturation tendency among the individual vineyards, and in alcohol, acid, tannin and anthocyanin content in the wines produced from them. Consequently, it has been possible to categorize vineyards according to tendency, and know which ones to look to for the raw material for the Union's several wines. Indeed the Union produces a wide range of wines relative to its total output, in order to make the best it can of three sorts of wine. Its total output usually ranges between 2,000 and 5,000 hectolitres yearly, although occasionally it reaches 7,000–8,000 hectolitres. Only 500–1,000 hectolitres become their appellation Amyntaion red wine. The Union would like to make a wine of still more limited production, but has no incentive for it at present. Usually, at least half of their output consists of dry and semi-dry rosé wines under the Astron label, which are also entitled to the appellation, as well as another red under that label which is not entitled, and an ordinary red and rosé under the Zephyr label. The remainder of their wine comprises sparkling wines produced by the closed-cuve method. The dry one labelled Amyntaion carries the appellation, while the dry and semi-dry ones under the Doukissa label do not. Neither the rosé nor the sparkling wines have any tradition in the region, but the better ones are entitled to the appellation in order to justify favourable prices to growers in unfavourable years, or on some less favourable plots, thereby keeping viticulture perennially attractive.

The red wine of Amyntaion was traditionally produced by a fermentation of the must on both stalks and skins for more than a month, which is still the method of peasant wine-makers, who prefer the more puckery sensation thus induced, a sensation which in any case tends to be pronounced in young red wines in this region because of the high acidity level the climate generally encourages; it is said that the *xynómavro* really justifies its name, 'sour/acid black', at Amyntaion. The Union, however, ferments the must on the skins alone for somewhat more than a week, the full fermentation lasting about three weeks. The result is a wine of 12° alcohol that matures more quickly than the traditional wine would. Nevertheless, Amyntaion red is only bottled after three years of maturation in oak; appellation rules require only one year. It is bottled with vintage indication, and marketed mostly in Macedonia and Athens.

THREE OF A KIND

The early nineteenth-century French traveller Boué called Naousa 'a red wine somewhat resembling Bordeaux with its acidity'. Well over a century later, the Greek enologist Georgakopoulos confirmed with laboratory data that there exists a most striking similarity between the detailed acid content of the Macedonian *xynómavro* wines and those of Bordeaux. That is not to say, however, that everyone tasting *xynómavro* wines will always think that Bordeaux is the correct association to make, not even if restricting the comparison to the feel of the wines. Some people find that the acidity in certain young Naousan wines today reminds them of one or another of the *grand crus* of Beaujolais. Other tasters think of certain Chiantis when they push Goumenissa wines about the mouth. But there was a reporter of the inter-war period who was reminded of Chianti by a Naousan wine. When tasting Amyntaion wines, some people make mention of the northernmost Italian reds, like Carema, perhaps in order to suggest an austerity of feel. As to the aromatics of *xynómavro* wines, thoughts turn in other directions. Greek enologists, among others, speak of *pinot noir*, an association that I am afraid will come to mind all the quicker after tasting the sparkling wines of Amyntaion. I have thought of certain Hungarian *kadarka* wines, such as Szekszárdi, in smelling some bottle-ready Naousan wines. Then there is the matter of colour, in which case none of the above associations will do. Rioja, perhaps, would make a pertinent comparison in that respect. One could almost think there is hardly any reason to have *xynómavro*, yet the fact is that when one gets down to a glass of these Macedonian wines, they defy comparison, which is saying quite a lot.

The appellation wines of Naousa hover over the dark cranberry range of redness, while the *káva* wines tend to be darker, though still fitting the Rioja association. But there are exceptions: Cava Vaeni, with its *cabernet* component, is noticeably darker than the others; Kava Melitzanis, with its five years in wood, seems to drop a lot of colour and is a light brick-red tinged with yellow; and Tsantalis's appellation wine Naousa has been unusually dark for an all-*xynómavro* wine since at least the 1984 vintage. Overall, Goumenissa wines are less deeply coloured than Naousan wines, and tend towards an orange tint at the rim at an earlier age. Amyntaion wine is the lightest of the group, being what the Greeks call 'red-black', with a slight orange tendency by bottling time in the case of the Union's Amyntaion red.

The relatively light colour of the *xynómavro* wines should not mislead about their feel, however. The *xynómavro* happens to yield quite tannic wine, but with a content of anthocyanins relatively low in relation to the tannin. Naousan wine in particular, while varying somewhat in body among samples, harbours a bold astringency that tends to look better in the rounder, fuller wines, especially Pigasos and Kava Khrisokhoou. Naousa is always firm wine, sometimes even bracing if given no bottle-age, and exerts quite a grip on the tongue, fitting its sensations over that organ like a glove. Goumenissa's wine is of relatively lighter body, and both softer in texture and less forceful. Amyntaion wine offers a particularly zesty quality that makes it seem as close to 'crisp' as we may legitimately speak of in relation to dry red wines suitable for bottle-ageing. The common aromatic aspect of the *xynómavro* wines seems to be an uncharted area between raspberry and strawberry jams and sweet potato. Allspice seems to be present too, at least in Kava Khrisokhoou, Pigasos and Grande Réserve Boutari, and floral smells come on with age in most cases. The best Naousan wines can be laid down advantageously for four to eight years, but perhaps longer as the vines gain some age, while those of Goumenissa and Amyntaion do not, in my experience, benefit by more than three to five years at best.

Having mistaken one of the *xynómavro* wines for another more than once – it can happen easily enough across vintages – perhaps I am not entitled to be very choosy on the matter of their matching to foods. Venturing where gourmet angels would fear to tread, I will nevertheless suggest that, in the pan-Hellenic kitchen, the Naousan wines should be tried with lamb *giouvétsi* or *kapamá*, a recent Kava Khrisokhoou or Pigasos with *mousaká*, Tsantalis's Naousa with *soudzoukákia*, Boutari's Goumenissa with *youvarlákia*, and Amyntaion with meat-stuffed vine leaves with *avgolémono* sauce. If familiarity of sensation is desired, Amyntaion ought to be taken with char-grilled steak, the Cooperative's Naousa with baked ham or roast pork, and Naousan wines generally with *coq au vin* and *bœuf bourgignon*, using the wine as confidently in the pot as on the table if one has a mind to. On the other hand there is something to be said for jettisoning all semblance of familiarity of sensation and going Cantonese instead: Amyntaion for beef with bok choy, Boutari's Goumenissa with beef chow foon, and Cava Vaeni with spare ribs in blackbean sauce. I shall close the list of possibilities by noting that Cousinéry, whom we know to have been as much given to qualitative distinctions as we are, complained not at all about having had to drink Naousan wine with trout at the lakeside in nearby Edessa.

SIATISTA

Situated about midway between Kozani and Grevena, on the south-western rim of the Vermio range, the town of Siatista lies hidden in a cleft in the south-facing slopes leading up to Mount Siniatsiko. Only the vineyards stretching out from that opening eastward towards Kozani alert the passing motorist for signs of settlement. The gravelly, limestone-dappled slopes might suggest that the vine has been cultivated at Siatista since time immemorial, although the town apparently grew into a wine centre only after the coming of the Ottomans. Earlier, Siatista, positioned at an altitude of about 970 metres, was no more than a small settlement of Vlakhs, a pastoral people of Latin speech. The late fifteenth-century influx of Greek-speaking refugees from more onerously governed places eventually resulted in the complete hellenization of Siatista, and with that a switch from animal husbandry to viticulture as the primary agricultural pursuit.

During the centuries of Ottoman rule, Siatista sold its wines in Macedonia and Thessaly, and was in the forefront of Ottoman wine-growing in the early nineteenth century: 'Each considerable owner has a wine-press, and there are cellars under all the larger houses, exhibiting the agreeable spectacle of butts, arranged in order , as in civilized Europe' (Leake, *Travels in Northern Greece*, 1835). Even today the visitor may visit Siatistan wine cellars and marvel nostalgically at their equipment. Perhaps no place in all of Greece has home cellars that announce so emphatically that the occupants have long meant business about wine. But the scene is one of a past plateau of technological excellence, rather as if it were frozen in time.

Since the late nineteenth century, Siatista has had practically no incentive to keep pace with wine-making advances. After phylloxera struck France, French merchants dusted off and cracked open the old travelogues and wine books, where they found mention of the town (Chatista or Schatista) in glowing terms; in a later edition of Jullien's book, Siatista's wines were called 'the best of Macedonia', just as they had been by Pouqueville. The merchants found their way there too, but of course had no interest in seeing the Siatistans bottle wine, or indeed that anything much should become of the place. They only wanted casks of the town's dry red wine with which to forge 'Bordeaux' back in France. The loss of that market after the French vineyards recovered was followed by phylloxera's attack on the town's own vineyards in 1926–8, and then by emigration, which has lasted down to the present time. Consequently, Siatista's wine-making facilities have never been substantially updated. Its enological development has seemingly atrophied irreversibly, and Siatista, once in the vanguard of wine-making, has become a backwater, dependent on furs for its continued survival. None the less it is possible to leave the town convinced that technological level is not always and everywhere an adequate indicator of wine quality.

Incredible as it may seem today, nearly 1,700 hectares of vines had spread across the clay-gravel inclines near Siatista in the early years of this century. They were planted mostly on the middle of the slopes, up to about 550 metres above sea level, hail being a very troublesome problem on the upper slopes. How sadly barren that tract looks now! Only around 100 hectares remain in production, and that very largely on the more easily worked lower slopes. The extra effort in planting and tending higher up is generally not deemed worth while, especially by the elderly people who do most of the vineyard work while those of their offspring who have remained behind prepare and peddle furs. Besides, the hazards for the Siatistan vintage are quite serious even on the lower slopes. Hail can thrash the fruit any time from late spring into early summer, and the climate, being wholly continental, can delay grape maturity menacingly. In any year the grapes are harvested late for Greece, not earlier than mid-October.

The English traveller Leake (1835) mentioned four Siatistan wines: a dry red, a dry white, a sweet white, and a wine flavoured with wormwood called *apsithinón*. All except the last are still made. Red wine is dominant, as it always has been, and made largely from *xynómavro*, which the Siatistans usually call *xynostáfylo*, or 'sour/acid grape'. Two other dark varieties grown to a small extent are *stavrotó* and *valándovo*. However, the variety of most special interest at Siatista is yet another one that is known as *moskhómavro*. Its name means 'musky black', yet it is not the 'black muscat' variety known in the West. The *moskhómavro* owes its significance to being the basis for Siatista's most highly regarded wine, the sweet *liastó*:

'The good reputation of the mutton and hare of Siatista is surpassed only by that of the wines, which, made in every house in its own way, reach their ultimate generosity in the *krasí iliastó*' (Leonhard Schultze, *Makedonien*, 1927). Early in this century, *liastó* was selling at ten times the price of the town's highly esteemed dry red.

In making *liastó*, *moskhómavro* is traditionally mixed with the other varieties, including *xynómavro*, but the proportion varies somewhat from cellar to cellar. Apart from this, the method of producing *liastó* is very much the same among all the Siatistan producers. The specially selected, well-ripened grapes are spread in the sun for about a week (hence the name *liastó*, and also that by which Leake called it, *liouménon*, both meaning 'sunned'), or else in airy rooms for about six weeks, depending on the weather and the availability of facilities. After losing approximately half their weight by dehydration, the grapes are crushed, and the mass of liquids and solids is passed through pouches of clean goat's wool. This process may have ancient origins: 'Question 7: Whether it is right to strain wine: ". . . those who draw off the impurities and unpalatable elements are simply tending and cleaning it" ' (Aristion, in Plutarch, *Moralia*, 'Table-talk'). The must is then put to ferment in small casks, sometimes of chestnut and sometimes of *róbolo*, a local pine-wood – sometimes it is actually called 'Roumeliote pine' or 'Macedonian pine' – although it does not give a piny flavour to *liastó*. After ten to fifteen days, the casks are closed and fermentation goes on for a further twenty-five to thirty days, at which time cold weather intervenes to impede the progress of the yeasts until about May the following year. Fermentation then recommences, and is allowed to come to a halt naturally, when the wine has reached $15–16°$ alcohol.

Two or three decades ago, six to seven years in cask was considered necessary for *liastó*. But nowadays producers who have some to sell find an ample profit in selling it at two to three years of age to the small coterie of Greeks who know about *liastó* and come looking for it. First of all, there is the colour to enthuse over. Leake described it as a white wine, as do the Siatistans, but its hue is a rare light amber shot with a variety of colours, including a certain budding pinkishness. *Liastó*'s colour is matched by the clarity of its bouquet which can justly be called phenomenal, although the facets of this aromatic gem are very difficult to identify individually. I might mention a certain nuance that is like ripe strawberries, but this seems too trite to do justice to such an uncommon wine. On the other hand

I might risk overdoing images of the exotic by mentioning guava paste. Better that I just describe the bouquet as an inextricable blend of unique fruity, nutty and floral aromas, and leave it at that ('the aim and object is not to make the mixture smell of one particular thing, but to produce a general scent derived from them all,' Theophrastus, *Concerning Odours*). Equally remarkable is the aromatic savour, *liastó* being as sheer on the mouth surfaces as any dessert wine might be and in no way distracting.

Far more stimulus than exists today is going to be required to replant the vineyards of Siatista and get *liastó* into bottle for common enjoyment. What hope there is seems at this time to rest with the Association of Viticulturalists of Siatista (*Sýllogos Ambelourgón Siátistas*), an organization which could in time become the nucleus of a cooperative association that would lead to a general rejuvenation of wine-growing at this most undeservedly obscure Macedonian town. In the meantime, visitors may contact the Association, possibly via the town hall (*dimarkhíon*), to gain entrée to the remaining Siatistan cellars.

KHALKIDIKI (CHALCIDICE)

Macedonia also has an Aegean front, most notably the three-pronged Khalkidiki peninsula projecting south and deep into the Aegean from east of Thessaloniki. The written record of the ancient Greeks, which perhaps is deficient on inland Macedonia, indicates that the most esteemed Macedonian vintages in antiquity were grown on Khalkidiki, especially at Mendi (Mende) and Skioni (Scione) on the southwestern part of the western prong called Kassandra, and at Akanthos (Acanthus) at the head of the eastern prong called Akti. In recent centuries, the best wine of Khalkidiki was considered to be that of Arnea, located in the east-central part of the peninsula's main sac. At present not of real commercial significance, the wine of Arnea is a dry red made from the ancient *limnió* variety, which has been the major grape variety of Khalkidiki in modern times, if not for some time earlier as well. Lately the *limnió*, with some outside help, is enjoying a revival on the peninsula generally, and has drawn Western attention to Khalkidiki, if sometimes for questionable reasons.

The locale that has been in the limelight is a 450-hectare vineyard estate near the community of Nea Marmaras, along the western rim of the middle prong of Khalkidiki, Sithonia, on which numerous vineyards were planted during ancient times. The estate belongs to the wealthy Carras family, who own the Porto Carras resort complex hard by it. Extending from 190–350 metres above sea level on hilly, sloping land of finely broken schist, the warm and dry Carras vineyard benefits from the proximity of the sea, as well as from an arc of pines enclosing it, which combine to moderate both warmth and dryness. The estate, which could be expanded by 100 hectares or so in coming years, was planted as from 1966 with both Greek and French grape varieties, selected to suit the environment, and actually planted in separate parcels, according to micro-environment, with the avowed intention of producing 'wines of European type'.

The rockier and drier southern part of the Carras estate was planted primarily with the Greek white varieties savatianó and rodítis, both brought from Attica, with the former growing on the poorer soils. The main exception in that area was the red cinsault. Red varieties were generally planted on the relatively richer soils of the more humid northern part of the estate, which is also its higher area, towards the pines. The limnió dominated in plantings there, followed by cabernet sauvignon and cabernet franc, as well as several other French varieties, mainly merlot, petit syrah and grenache. The Macedonian xynómavro was also planted, but proved to be outside the environmental zone in which it really succeeds. In addition, the Greek white varieties athíri and asýrtiko, respectively brought from Rhodes and Santorini, were planted in the north, and so were smaller areas of sauvignon blanc and ugni blanc. On the basis of a decade of experience in growing and vinifying the several varieties, an appellation of origin was authorized for the Carras estate in 1981, under the unlikely Greek name 'Playies Melitona', which translates as the distinctly French 'Côtes de Meliton'. 'Meliton' refers to the mount on whose slopes the estate is planted. The regulation specifies red wines composed of 70 per cent limnió and 15 per cent each of the two cabernets, and white wines of 50 per cent athíri, 35 per cent rodítis, and 15 per cent asýrtiko. The percentages only became compulsory in 1989.

About 900 hectolitres of wine are produced annually at the Carras estate, of which about half is appellation white wine on the Domaine Carras label, which up until now has been made from asýrtiko (30 per cent), athíri (30 per cent), rodítis (20 per cent), sauvignon blanc (10 per cent), and ugni blanc (10 per cent). A white Carras Reserve, now also bearing the appellation, has been composed of *asýrtiko* and *sauvignon blanc* in a ratio of 7:3, and produced in a quantity of about 100 hectolitres annually. Three reds have borne the appellation: Domaine Carras, which is from a mix of *cabernet sauvignon* and *limnió*; Cava Carras, an all-*cabernet sauvignon* entry; and Château Carras, made from 30 per cent each of the two *cabernets* and *limnió*, plus *merlot*. They are produced in quantities of, respectively, about 150, 120 and 40 hectolitres annually. Cava Carras and Château Carras spend two to four years in bottle before being marketed, in addition to eighteen to twenty months in barrel, and are *vins de garde*, especially Château Carras. But the quicker-maturing Domaine Carras has its own charms, even at six to seven years of age, with a special character all its own. A Carras Rosé Special is also made mostly from *limnió, cinsault* and *merlot*. It will be noticed that both the red and the white Domaine Carras wines are closest in make-up to what the appellation regulations call for. Presumably, the composition will have to change if the appellation is to be retained after 1989, in order not to give the impression of a cosy relationship between the Carras family and the Ministry of Agriculture.

The general resemblance of the Carras wines to Western European prototypes has won the Carras project the plaudits of Western wine commentators, some of whom are quite lavish in their praise, suggesting the wines as the best of Greece, and the project as the most interesting in Greek wine. However that may be, the sensibilities of at least a few Greek wine professionals are offended by the Carras philosophy. They cannot conceive of Greek wine that does not spring directly from a local populace and its habits, and worry that Greece is all too prone to relinquish its own heritage in wine for the sake of catering to the taste of a Western clientele, becoming rather like what one detractor of the Carras project calls 'a water-carrier to Europe'. Maybe it is not too late to hope, however, that a real local tradition will evolve as fruitfully as happened when the French landed in Rioja, but I think that would require greater recognition of the remarkable *limnió*.

East of Sithonia, the Akti arm of Khalkidiki has become the source of wines related to those from the Carras estate, though perhaps with some greater claim to indigenous tradition. Akti is for all practical purposes synonymous with Mount Athos, or Ayion Oros (Holy Mountain), the pan-Orthodox community of all-male monasteries. Vineyards proliferated on Athos after the Ottomans came to power and the monasteries there lost the lands that they had held elsewhere. The vines planted were primarily *limnió*, but also included varieties brought by monks from the Black Sea coast of Georgia. The Georgian varieties were appreciated for their resistance to disease, easy cultivation and high yields. However, they were not of *vinifera* type, and their fruit displayed the so-called 'foxy' aroma associated with *labrusca*, etc. The monks therefore typically diluted the Georgian flavour with *limnió*. The best wine of Athos, however, was considered to be varietal *limnió* from the 'Monoxylitis' vineyard belonging to the Monastery of Ayios Dionysius, directly below Ayion Oros proper.

The Tsantalis firm reached an agreement with the monks whereby several of the same varieties grown at the Carras estate were planted, in addition to more of the *limnió* already at Athos. The locale used is that called Khromitsa, belonging to the lands of the Russian Monastery of Ayios Panteleimonas. About 6,000 hectolitres of Tsantalis's red and white Ayioritiko wines are produced each year. Though not an appellation of origin, the Ayioritiko name, which indicates 'Ayion Oros', has been authorized since 1981 as a legal *vin de pays* designation for red and white wines with the same respective varietal make-up as their counterparts from Playies Melitona, except that in the case of the red, *cabernet sauvignon* and *cabernet franc* may be in any proportion as long as together they comprise 30 per cent. As with Playies Melitona, the varietal proportions for both the red and the white wine became compulsory only in 1989. A red Ayioritiko from *limnió*, *fokianó* and other red varieties grown at Monoxylitis has lately been offered by the little Protopapas winery.

THRACE

Thus far, Greece's 'pan-handle' region of Thrace, to the east of Macedonia, has not participated in the growing Greek trend towards bottling wine. Thrace is perhaps just a bit too far away from Greece's main population centres to be encouraged to develop wine-growing. Moreover, the region proved to have such outstanding conditions for oriental tobacco cultivation, that the vine has generally been unable to compete, although some land is otherwise quite suitable for it. Even prior to the vogue for smoking, however, the rural Moslem population, which is still found in many places, had kept Thrace poor in vineyards during recent centuries. Inhabitants of the

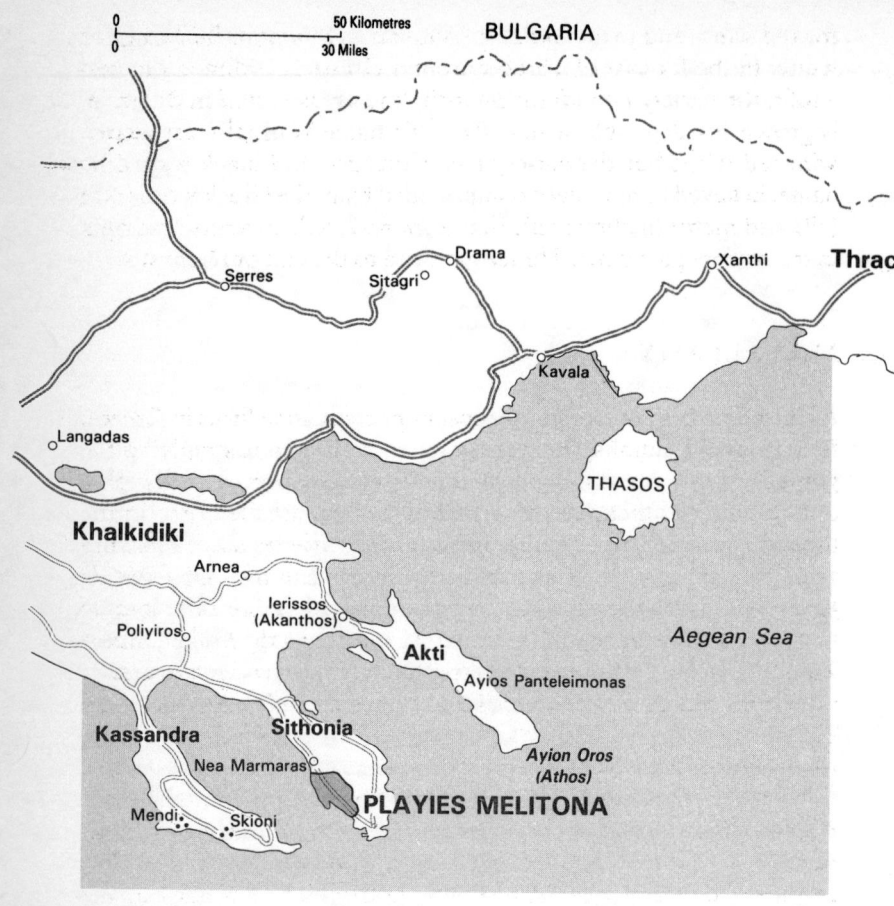

Eastern Macedonia and Western Thrace

towns of Aegean Thrace were largely supplied with quality wine by the northerly islands of the Archipelago, especially Thasos and Bozcaada (Tenedos), or from places now in adjacent Bulgaria, such as Asenovgrad, and Turkey, like Kirklareli.

Despite the historical hindrances to the development of commercial wine-growing in Thrace, a local reputation was enjoyed by wines from the hills north-west of Xanthi, where the *mavroúdi Thrákis*, or 'blackie of Thrace', which is probably a clone of the *mavrud* variety grown across the Rodopi Mountains at Asenovgrad, is prominent for red wine, and the *zoumiátiko*, known as *dimiat* in Bulgaria, for white. In the far east of Thrace, around Orestias, Didimotikho and Soufli, the variety *pamídi* (or *pamíti*), known as *pamid* in Bulgaria, is grown for dry table wines. *Pamídi*'s name is usually associated with red wine, but the variety has white, red and black forms. Its name, believed to have been compounded from the Greek words *pan* (all) and *méthi* (inebriation), that is *'pamméthi'*, suggests an origin in the remote past when Thrace gave rise to the cult of Dionysus.

MISCELLANY

As the home base of two of the most important wine firms in Greece, Boutari and Tsantalis, the north-eastern mainland is supplying the grapes for a number of wines that have no very precise geographic origin. Some of them are nevertheless 'typical' of the north in the broadest way, usually because of the grape varieties used. In future years, several may serve as a basis for instituting respective *vin de pays* (*topikós ínos*) categories, and be improved as a result. Notable in that regard are the red and white wines sold under the Makedonikos Tsantali label, which are made, respectively, from *xynómavro* grapes of various places and *zoumiátiko* of Serres and Nea Ankhialos by Thessaloniki, as well as Roditis Tsantali, a rosé wine made from *rodítis* grapes grown at Mesemvria and the same Nea Ankhialos.

More eclectic wines are also offered by Boutari and Tsantalis. Rosé Boutari, once an all-*xynómavro* wine, first of Ayios Panteleimonas near Amyntaion, and then of west-central Macedonia at large, has become a blend of *xynómavro* with *ayioryítiko* of Nemea in the Peloponnesos. It is a very slightly off-dry rosé. The dry red Cava Boutari has always been a half-and-half mix of *xynómavro* of the Naousa area and Nemean *ayioryítiko*. It is aged in oak for at least four years and released in vintage-dated bottles. Cava Boutari is a boon to tourists in that it is easily found in half-bottles virtually throughout Greece, and sells sufficiently fast for it always to show as its producer would wish. Tsantalis offers a dry red wine that is a half-and-half mix of *xynómavro* from the Naousa area and *cabernet sauvignon* from Khalkidiki, called Cava Tsantali. Actually it is the firm's reserve red wine, produced in a quantity of about 2,000 hectolitres annually. Full in body and somewhat fleshy in texture when at its best, Cava Tsantali is remarkable for presenting decided character in spite of its mixed origin, and vivid proof that the Greeks have not entirely lost their touch as mixers:

> [A beneficial] result also follows, it is said, from the mixture of different wines – for example, if a strong fragrant wine be mixed with one that is mild and without fragrance (for instance, if the wine of Heraclea be mixed with the wine of Erythrae), since the latter contributes its mildness and the former its fragrance: for the effect is that they simultaneously destroy one another's inferior qualities through the mildness of the one and the fragrance of the other. There are many other such blends mentioned by and known to experts.
>
> (Theophrastus, *Concerning Odours*)

CLASSICAL REFLECTIONS

Some evidence from northern Greece suggests that the ancients' sophisticated debate over wine's relationship to fire and water, which in a real sense was a probing of the question of 'balance', was intricately bound up with the earliest notions pertaining to the nature of Dionysus.

Several of the Greek writers addressed the question of whether wine is 'hot' or 'cold', that is, whether it belongs to the element of fire or water. Noticing both that fermentation engenders 'heat' (or 'seething'), and that wine causes 'heating' in the body, the ancients generally attributed wine's essential nature to fire. On the other hand, however, Plato (*Timaeus*) mentioned wine as a kind of water that had passed through the plants of earth, while Aristotle (*Meteorologica*) observed that wines to a greater or lesser extent behave like watery liquids, in that they evaporate. Furthermore, the ancients also noticed that the sweat provoked by wine 'cools' the body. Plutarch concluded that 'wine is not hot in an absolute sense' (*Moralia*, 'Table-talk), and in another context suggests that that is just as well since 'fire without moisture is unsustaining and arid', just as 'water without heat is unproductive and inactive' (*Moralia*, 'The Roman Questions'). The yang/yin relationship of the two is also discernible in the Dionysian legends: 'The ethereal flame [Zeus's 'fiery bolt'] blazed with livelier sparks through the water of the torrents which struck it; the thirsty water boiled and steamed, and the liquid essence dried up in the red-hot mass' (Nonnos, *Dionysiaca*).

In eastern Macedonia, south-west of the town of Drama, a prehistoric site called Sitagri has yielded grape seeds whose conformation positively dates grape varieties approximating to the modern cultivated type to as early as the third millennium BC. Significantly, the site is on an artificially drained plain. This strongly suggests that the earliest vine-tenders regarded ample water as a requisite for successful cultivation of the vine. Their judgement had probably originated in their having noticed that the wild vine grew near springs, streams and other relatively wet places where natural vegetation flourished, since it was apparently that same observation which suggested to them a means of propping up vines:

> 'Spare me, Dionysus, the river-fed from Zeus! Be gracious to my fertilizing waters! for your own goodly fruitage of grapes has grown up from water. I have sinned, Dionysus, nurseling of fire! . . . Destroy not my canes, the growth of my streams, which grow up to support the shoots and grapes of your vine! Do not the reeds tied together carry your well-watered fruit?'
>
> (The nymph Hydapses, in Nonnos's *Dionysiaca*)

Hence too was it related that Hermes had given 'in charge of the daughters of Lamos, river nymphs – the son of Zeus, the vineplanter' Dionysus (*Dionysiaca*). Dionysus's transformation from a god of vegetative growth into a god of the vine could also be explained by the vine's early association with riparian environments.

North-east of Thessaloniki, at the village of Langadas, Greeks relocated from the vicinity of the Black Sea coast in eastern Thrace earlier in this century observe a rite known as the *anastenária*, beginning on 2 May, the Feast of SS Constantine and Helen. Thrace was the source of the Dionysian cult, and the *anastenária*, although long ago christianized, is considered linked by its particulars to true bacchanalia. Among its features are intemperate drinking and the ceremonial slaughter of animals, but the most striking part of the celebration is a barefooted romp on live coals by ecstatic dancers, who suffer no burns in consequence. The circumstance of the dance constitutes perhaps the most telling evidence of the symbolic link between fire, Dionysus and wine in the mind of the early Aegean wine drinker.

Mythology told that Dionysus's mother, Semele, was set afire by

Zeus's thunderbolt when she asked him to reveal his glory, and that while she burned Zeus took the child and sewed it into his leg until it was ready for birth. Consequently, 'the weapon of Dionysus is fire, because it is his father's and comes from the thunderbolt' (Lucian, *Dionysus*). If the myth was not something in the way of a metaphor recommending a Zeus-fearing approach to wine – and perhaps also one intimating an 'unnatural' aspect of the thirst for it – the custom of the *anastenária* dancers in any case seems to reflect a tacit belief that even if Dionysus stood with his feet in water he could be a hothead all the same. 'He set Bacchus more in a flame, since wine excites the mind for desire, and wine finds unbridled youth much more obedient to the rein when it is charmed with the prick of unreason' (Nonnos, *Dionysiaca*).

GASTRONOMIC NOTES

The inland part of northern Greece was marked not merely by certain regional specialities but also by a dietary pattern that separated it from the Aegean world. It could be called Greece's 'continental cuisine', and marked a transition from the Aegean to the central Balkans. While the Aegean area relied on olive oil for fat all year round, the northerly mainland areas used olive oil principally in warm weather and during religious fasting periods, buying the oil from coastal merchants. During the rest of the year, animal fats were customary. Sheep's-milk butter was widely used in the summer, while sheep's suet was typical of late autumn and early winter. In some parts of the far north, pork fat was predominant. Similarly, the consumption of meat by type was also highly seasonal, although in any season meat consumption was greater than in the Aegean. The traditional pattern was lamb in spring and early summer, poultry in late summer, pork in early winter, mutton in late winter, and game throughout the colder months. Beef, however, was not typical of any season, but instead was only an occasional meat, usually available when work animals had been slaughtered. Preserved meats were also very popular and commonplace, especially in the colder weather. Two favourites were *soudgioútsia*, sausages of pork or beef, and *bastourmá*, a smoked meat, usually of sheep or goat.

Traditional northern main courses tend to be meat-heavy compared to their Aegean counterparts. They are generally subsumed under one of three headings: *giouvétsi, kebáb* and *stamnáki. Giouvétsi*, which is named for the open ceramic vessel in which it is baked, is most often a mix of meat and vegetables, although in warm weather possibly a phantasmagoria of fresh vegetables. In any case, northern *giouvétsi* is not to be identified with the pan-Hellenic pot of pasta and meat which goes by that name. *Kebáb* is not usually a skewered preparation, but rather a sort of ragoût stewed in a pan with onion and assorted flavourings. The meat is cut into little pieces to be picked up with a fork, hence the connection with the skewered specialities. *Stamnáki* (little jug) refers to the small-mouthed earthenware container, apparently akin to the ancient *stámnos*, in which a stew is baked under a lid sealed with a dough of flour and water. *Stamnáki* used to be known also by the Turkish-sounding term *tsoblék-kebab* (jug kebab), which again attests to bite-size chunks of meat.

Among the vast repertoire of variations on the three main-course themes, the one that seems to have survived regularly in the cuisine of the *tavérna*, is *tás-kebab*. It is made in a pan, with small chunks of beef or pork, onion, bay leaf, a touch of hot paprika, and perhaps a dash of cinnamon. Olive oil rather than suet serves as the cooking fat nowadays. Traditional northerners must be scandalized by what usually goes under the name *tás-kebab* elsewhere in Greece, good though those dishes may be. Try with *tás-kebab* a newly bottled Kava Khrisokhoou or Pigasos. More unusual, and most rare now – it is hardly to be encountered in the usual town *tavérna* even in its season – is *kavourmás-kebab*, made from pieces of *kavourmás*, which is the Macedonian version of *confit*: pieces of mutton kept in their fat in a sheep's stomach. Drink with it whatever may be available.

In the more northern reaches of Macedonia and Thrace, typically Mediterranean vegetables like aubergine, okra and artichoke were scarcely known before this century. Similarly, the tomato, which was widely adopted in Aegean cooking by the nineteenth century, remained unusual in parts of Macedonia and Thrace until the early twentieth century. Instead, the north had a particular partiality for leek, the gourd-like squashes, and cabbage. Savoury pastries, or *pítes*, filled with leek or squash mixtures were very popular, and both Naousa and Siatista were famous for them, even exporting them to distant towns. Sour cabbage was also known. The area around Kastoria in western Macedonia still makes *armiópita*, a *píta* with a sour cabbage filling; its name is a contraction of *almyrí píta*, which might be rendered in English as 'brine pie'. Choose Amyntaion red to go with it. A sweetish *píta* typical of Macedonia and Thrace is *kolokithópita*, which might be described, however roughly, as a sort of pumpkin strudel. If you can contrive to, drink a glass of Siatista's *liastó* with it.

An important native seasoning is parsley. The Greek names for it are *magdanós* and *makedonísi*, both of which attest to the popular belief that Macedonia is the original provenance of the herb. Parsley appears – or at least it used to appear – as a major flavouring in many dishes. The capsicum family of spice, although not indigenous, has long been known in northern Greece, having spread like wildfire after its introduction in areas of Turkish population. One such area was between Amyntaion and Goumenissa, which today produces virtually all Greek paprika. The centre of production is Aridea. Visitors to Macedonia in the nineteenth century noted the use of paprika in cooking, but other pungent spices were also known, though sweet ones like cinnamon and cloves were not used so often or so emphatically as in the Aegean. Cumin was especially popular in preserved meats. Saffron was also known in Macedonia, and even grown in some places. Herbs and spices were often pounded into composite mixtures, or with still other ingredients into spreads, generically called *piperítsa*, to be used mostly as condiments for bread. *Piperítsa* offers remarkable improvisational opportunities for complementing a wine's aromatic character.

7
Thessaly

In Thessaly there are some excellent growths [crus] on the slopes of Pelion and Ossa, as at Ambelakia, in the valley of Tempe, as well as at the foot of the mountain, toward Farsala, to the north of Trikala, and below the monasteries of Meteora, near Kalambaka.
(Ami Boué, French traveller, *La Turquie d'Europe*, 1840)

Set in the middle of continental Greece, the region of Thessaly sprawls out across a monotonous and fertile plain whose flatness would seem to show little promise wine-wise. In fact, Thessaly's agricultural renown has always rested on its large output of field crops, as attested by archaeological finds that go back to times long before the evidence of written records. Thessaly was Greece's granary during antiquity, and in that regard is second only to much larger Macedonia today. Yet the vine grows wild in parts of Thessaly and viticulture is an ancient branch of farming in the region. A few Thessalian wines may have been well regarded in antiquity, though perhaps mostly ones grown on the periphery of the plain. Thessaly is bounded by mountains and sea, which afford it environments altogether suited to yielding excellent wine. Those areas have been used for wine-growing in recent centuries, and several are at present being tapped for the Greek market. The results with several bottled wines are most encouraging for the future.

RAPSANI

Just before it enters the Vale of Tempe, the National Highway (*Ethnikí Odós*) leading from Thessaloniki south to Athens jags through the south-eastern foothills of Olympus, and in the area

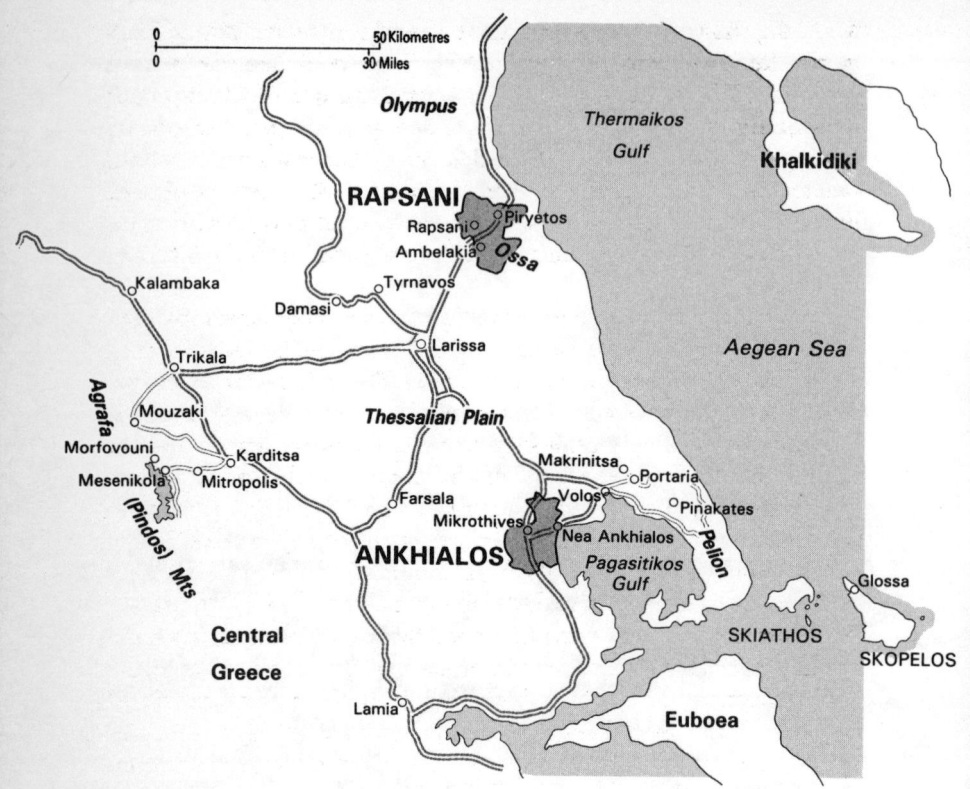

Thessaly

around Mount Kissavos, the ancient Ossa, passes near the vineyards producing Rapsani, the sole Thessalian red wine currently entitled to an appellation of origin, and traditionally one of the most touted of the mainland. Vineyards may have been planted on Kissavos in ancient times, but, if so, they were not precisely those of Rapsani. Founded in the late fifteenth century, the village is another living monument to the Ottoman occupation, when refugees fled out of sight, into the mountains. Ever since its settlement, Rapsani has been the chief wine village of the area, and today supplies 80–90 per cent of the raw material grown in the appellation zone. The only other villages of this tiny wine district are neighbouring Piryetos, Krania and Ambelakia. Excepting Piryetos, which was in the thrall of Turkish and Greek landlords until around the time of the First World

War, they have a long tradition of interdependence, dating back to the late eighteenth century, when Ambelakia became a most prominent Thessalian town, owing to its manufacture and export of high-quality yarn, which spawned a cooperative-like production unit linking the three villages. The demise of the yarn trade in the nineteenth century plunged Ambelakia into obscurity, and then into decline as a settlement. Once a substantial producer of wine, Ambelakia, whose name means 'Little Vineyards', is quite insignificant now.

Earlier in this century, before phylloxera and emigration took their toll, about 500 hectares of vines were cultivated in the Rapsani area. At present, the total is about 300 hectares. The vineyards are situated mostly in the range of 300–500 metres above sea level, and generally face south-east. The juxtaposition of the Olympus massif and the Aegean Sea creates a delicate climatic situation: while the influence of Olympus works towards lowering air temperature, exposure to the Aegean environment has a contrary influence. The result is that the Rapsani vintage is one of the most quixotic on the mainland for the wine-grower to contend with. Too much of a swing one way or the other during the growing season skews the character of the vintage, especially towards excessive malic acid and somewhat severe wine if the weather is too cool, and highly alcoholic yet thin wine if too warm. Of special concern is the *lívas*, the very warm, dry southwesterly wind that blows through the Tempe Gorge in summer, and which can rob the fruit of needed moisture. Some protection from the *lívas* is afforded by the ample autumn and winter precipitation that characterizes the Olympus area, and seeps down through Kissavos further into the year, nourishing, but not collecting in, the calcareous land on which the Rapsani vineyards are planted.

Mostly, three dark grape varieties are grown around Rapsani: *xynómavro, stavrotó* (also called *ambelakiótiko* locally) and *krasáto*. The varietal complement apparently reflects geographic location. Rapsani is the southernmost major traditional site of the Macedonian *xynómavro*, while also one of the more northerly sites of the *stavrotó*, which in spite of having the synonym 'Ambelakiote' is thought to have originated on Euboea, off the Thessalian coast to the south-east. Only the *krasáto* is considered native to the general area around Kissavos. Whatever its lineage, the *krasáto* evokes ancient associations by its name alone, which means 'wine-coloured'. The term frequently occurs in classical literature as a description of the range of colour from purple to bluish-black, though in the classical Greek terms *ínops (oenops)* (wine-looking) and *inódis (oenodis)* (winy), the latter as in Homer's 'wine-dark sea'. Curiously then, if the *krasáto* looks 'wine-dark' on the vine, it is actually relatively lacking in the anthocyanins that give violet colour to deeply red wines, and needs to be vinified with other varieties in order for the colour of its wine to be darkened and intensified. However, while the appellation regulation for Rapsani wine requires the use of all three of the named varieties, no proportion is specified. Traditionally, village habits in the latter regard have varied. Indeed at Ambelakia the *stavrotó* has always been the most favoured variety, and is sometimes used to the near-exclusion of the other two varieties, or else with a fourth red sort, the *limnió* (called *limnióna* locally).

Nearly 1,000 tons of grapes are harvested from the Rapsani vintage in an average year. About 300–400 tons of that is processed by the Wine Production Cooperative of Rapsani. Although it is the major producer of Rapsani wines, the Cooperative buys a relatively small share of local grape production, owing to its stipulation that the vineyards from which it buys must be planted one-third to each of the varieties required by the appellation rules; hence Ambelakia, so heavily given over to *stavrotó*, sells less to the Cooperative than even Piryetos and Krania. The measure is intended to enhance wine quality by assuring evenness of quality in the purchased grapes of the three varieties. Also, the Cooperative hopes that by offering higher prices for qualifying grapes, they will encourage local growers to plant in a corresponding manner, thereby enabling production of a greater quantity of wine in the future. They are not fully able to stimulate and guide development of the Rapsani region as they see fit, though. Their winery, which sits alongside the National Highway near the turn-off for the village of Rapsani, belongs, not to the Cooperative, but to the Agricultural Bank of Greece, which financed its construction and has kept it under its not always very green thumb ever since. The Cooperative is not particularly pleased by the situation, feeling that the Bank, an interloper in the region, so to speak, retards the area's viticultural revival. They hope to take over control completely in the future.

The vintage at Rapsani takes place in late September. Fermentation of the must is on skins only, for about one month; home-made wines are fermented on stalks as well. Between 60 and 70 per cent of the grapes delivered to the Cooperative become appellation wine, or about 1,200–2,000 hectolitres annually, to be bottled under the Rapsani label. It is a 12.5° wine, bottled after at least three years in oak. Appellation regulations specify a minimum of only one year, which seems rather optimistic in view of the usual need – even in an ideal vintage – for an extensive malolactic, or secondary, fermentation. The Cooperative also produces two other wines: Rosso, one of the best second-line red wines in Greece; and an unusual and savoury rosé called Bella Rosa.

A second producer of Rapsani wine is Mitrakos Brothers, whose annual production has varied from 50–100 hectolitres since they began bottling in 1982. Their wine, called Kentavros (Centaur), is produced entirely from grapes bought from a select few wine-growers around Rapsani, but may not carry an appellation since it is vinified outside the Rapsani zone, at Pournari, to the south near Larisa. Mitrakos Brothers also vinify the three requisite varieties in approximately equal proportion. Kentavros usually spends at least eighteen months in barrel, but more time is given to those wines chosen to be designated further by a 'Réserve Spéciale' neck label. It is planned that in the best years the entire output will justifiably be bottled with that distinction. In lesser years, only those barrels whose contents meet rigorous objective (measurable) and sensory standards will be marketed as 'Réserve Spéciale'. For instance, only one barrel from the first vintage for which the designation was used, 1984 – a very good one – met them. In some years, too, there will be none. The 'Réserve Spéciale' is marked especially by very formidable body and 13.5–14.5° alcohol. The plain Kentavros is considerably lighter and at 12.5°, generally, it is in all respects more like the Cooperative's appellation wine, which should by no means be overlooked.

Among Greek red wines coming from appellation regions, I have found none so radically divergent, one from the other, as Rapsani and Kentavros 'Réserve Spéciale'. Bottle-ready Rapsani varies in colour from dark copper with full onion-skin tones at the rim, to a particular orange-red which only some manufacturers of children's wax crayons seem to reproduce. Kentavros, on the other hand, is a blackish-red trying to pass for mahogany. Other features of the two wines are in no less striking contrast. The bouquet of Rapsani combines something of berries with more of plums, and perhaps still more of stewed rhubarb. And yet none of that manages to submerge an aspect I have heard likened, with some reason, to the Middle Eastern eggplant-sesame-lemon creation, *baba ghanouj*. Kentavros is evocative of the aromas of leather and tobacco, but somehow, I also spot the humble celery seed in there – in the nicest way, to be sure. In the finish, Rapsani is marked by an emphatic vigour of after-taste featuring a healthy, citrus-like tang, and a rinsing of the palate which at times seems to occur quite literally 'in waves', while Kentavros trails off like the biggest and grandest kind of Barolo imaginable.

Nor have I ever so utterly despaired of finding a straight answer to the intrusive question, so disruptive of enjoyment, as to which of two wines is a more worthy representative of their region. While I would have to concede a conventional superiority to the eminently age-worthy Kentavros 'Réserve Spéciale', I have never been able to pour off the last glass from a bottle of Rapsani without feeling profoundly grateful that it is as it is. What might otherwise be disparaged as a certain 'roughness' has in Rapsani been raised to a virtue worthy of Olympus and its gambolling, vying, almost flesh-and-blood deities whom I expect would be sorely disappointed with any drink we mortals might call 'divine' or 'heavenly'. More than any other sort of red wine I have come upon, Rapsani's feel has demonstrated to me why the Greeks would have applied their word *kharaktír* to a wine: 'character' literally indicates a 'notching'. Do not make the mistake of treating this rolling stone as though it were one of our moss-gathering wines. Be sure to drink it within a couple of years of its bottling, before it has lost its splendid nerve and inimitable, arresting display of 'harmony-in-motion'.

Owing to its finish, Rapsani may please many who normally would not choose a red of more than light-medium body as a pre-dinner wine. The persistent crackling sensations of appetizers like *tyrópita* and *spanakotyrópita* triangles provide a curious counterweight to the wine's finish. Bitterish morsels, like olives, are accommodated, and so are frankly salty titbits. Well-herbed *souvláki* is a good choice for more substantial snacks, although I would not claim it superior to pastrami on rye. If bringing a bottle home from holiday, one should not neglect poultry dishes in which the crisp, browned skin of the bird figures as a prize morsel, whether Cantonese roast duck with Chinese broccoli, Peking duck, or, more mundanely, chicken glazed with honey. A grand accompaniment is minced rabbit and spinach *en croûte* with Dijon sauce. Kentavros 'Réserve Spéciale' gets my approval for the heartiest stews, casseroles, and game dishes.

ANKHIALOS

Thessaly also has an appellation of origin entitlement for a white wine, produced at Ankhialos, a seaside community of Magnisia located a few miles south of Thessaly's port city of Volos, on the Pagasitikos Gulf. Included in the boundaries of the appellation zone are vineyards of the name-giving place, which is by far the major source of grapes, as well as Mikrothives, the only other significant producer, and, nominally, Aïdinio and Krokki. The appellation entitlement specifies dry white wine of at least 85 per cent *rodítis* grapes and the remainder *savatianó*, two white varieties which respectively occupy about 75 and 10 per cent of the nearly 400 hectares of vines planted.

Several additional requirements pertain to the production of appellation Ankhialos wine. All of the grapes must be grown on unsupported vines, since those trained on cordons in this area yield four times as much fruit, and wine of palpably lesser quality. Also, none of the slightly reddish colour in the skin of *rodítis* grapes grown at Ankhialos may be picked up by the wine. Traditionally in the area, some household producers encourage a rosy tint by fermenting on the skins a few days. The stipulation for the appellation wine is motivated in part because the variety concerned is the white *rodítis*, and in part because tannins that would be imparted to the wine along with colour would detract from 'freshness'. Also with the aim of achieving freshness, the wine must not come into contact with wood. The extra expense entailed by the latter provision hinders individual growers who might otherwise care to attempt to produce and bottle an appellation wine. None is soon likely to refurbish and compete with the local Dimitra Cooperative, which is producing a very good appellation wine, under the Anchialos label. It is a 90 per cent *rodítis* wine bottled about six months after the vintage, with vintage indication. The first bottling was in 1983 (1982 vintage), in an amount of 1,000 hectolitres, compared to Dimitra's total output of 40,000 hectolitres. More Anchialos is planned for future years.

The nature of Anchialos owes a great deal to its origin in a very low-lying wine district which fronts on to the sea. Most of its vineyards are in the range of about 100 metres above sea level, and some go right down to the water's edge, though few of these qualify for appellation wine because they are mostly cordon-trained. None of the vineyards goes above the 200-metre mark – most of those are found at Mikrothives. Because of the proximity of the sea, and especially its saturation of the local soil, a notable characteristic of Anchialos is a very high level of dry extract, but particularly sodium chloride. Attributed to that is an impression of medium body that the wine's alcohol alone, at 11.5°, would be unlikely to leave. The particular make-up of extract content is also credited with a most unusual sensation: an immediate, intense and long-lasting drying feel on the forward upper surface of the tongue. Yet neither fruitiness nor freshness is lacking, or at least not while the wine is within a year or so of the vintage date and holds its silvery greenish-straw colour. The barest carbonic sensation provides a certain sprightliness as well.

For accompanying Anchialos, this most unusual white wine, I would especially recommend any kind of salted crisp served with guacamole dip, and relatively plain foods that can be served with sour cream or yogurt, such as potato pancakes or meatless stuffed grapevine leaves. Despite its seaside birthplace, Anchialos has not impressed me as having a special affinity for seafood, though one day I may smuggle a flask of it into my favourite sushi bar, where it can meet up with its element in the raw.

Other wines of the Dimitra Cooperative also convey pelagic notions of vinous harmony. Prominent among them is the dry white Nymphe, formerly their flagship wine. A lesser white is Lefkos Xiros ('White Dry'). Its red counterpart, Erythros Xiros ('Red Dry'), is produced from the *sykiótis*, a black variety occupying about 15 per cent of vineyard land around Ankhialos. As one might expect of a red wine grown in this area, Erythros Xiros is nearly parching, even though it is not remarkably tannic at all. Dimitra's Retsina, a wine with virtually no tradition in Thessaly except in some areas adjacent to Central Greece, perhaps qualifies as the really quintessential Greek wine: product of vine, pine and brine.

KARDITSA-AGRAFA

One of the larger vineyard areas of Thessaly is situated all the way inland, due west of Volos, and centred around the large country town of Karditsa. A majority of the nearly 1,600 hectares of vines is planted in proximity to the town itself, but all fall within the nomarchy of Karditsa. Consequently, the bottled wines being produced in the area, all by the Union of Agricultural Cooperatives of Karditsa, tend to be identified as 'Karditsa wine'. In a very real sense, however, two quite distinct wine regions are subsumed under that name. The one comprises the level fields of vines around Karditsa, which are surrounded by far more fields of crops. Mostly dessert or dual-purpose grapes are grown: *moskháto amvoúrgou* (muscat of Hamburg); *batíki*, which is a sort commonly found in Thessaly, but originally brought from Asia Minor; *rozakí*; and *fráoula*. Plantings of strictly wine grape varieties are quite in the minority, and a very large portion of those is *savatianó*.

The other vineyard zone of Karditsa consists of the villages of Agrafa, the latter name being that applied to the mountains in the south-east of the Pindos range. Agrafa has had a somewhat peculiar history for an area in the centre of the mainland. It escaped the reach of spreading feudalism in Byzantine times because its terrain and meagre lands for farming were not conducive to the easy imposition of land concentration that took place on the plain. Later, the Agrafa villages offered sufficient armed resistance to the Ottomans to persuade the conquerors that this particular conquest was not worth their while, so that the lands there were never collected up into fiefdoms as on the plain. The peasants were thus left free to cultivate whatever they were wont to, and most maintained vineyards.

The most important wine villages of Agrafa are Mesenikola, Moskhato, Morfovouni and Mitropoli, while a lesser role is played by Ayios Yeoryios, Xynoneri, Mouzaki, Paliouri and Dafnospilia. Their vineyards are primarily planted with wine grape varieties, including *savatianó* in post-phylloxera times, but featuring the *mávro mesenikóla* (Mesenikola black), which will probably gain Karditsa – not Agrafa – an appellation of origin entitlement within a few years' time. Despite its name, which would appear to stake a firm claim to indigenous origin, the *mávro mesenikóla* is mentioned in local lore as having been brought to Agrafa from Western Europe in Ottoman times, by a certain Monsieur Nicolas (*Mesenikóla*) who lent his name first to the village, and through that to the grape. However that may be, the *mávro mesenikóla* became the most highly regarded variety on Agrafa, and was extensively planted. Nevertheless, only about 100 hectares of the variety are cultivated today, owing to the decline in vineyard area that was caused by the arrival of phylloxera in the late 1920s, as well as the post-Second World War population exodus. The vineyards are located primarily in the range of 250–600 metres above sea level, which roughly comprises the semi-mountainous zone, but also reach Lake Tavropos, or Megdova, at 800 metres. The utilized land is mostly sloping, except at Mitropoli and Xynoneri, where level land is more usual.

The leading wine of the Union is Erato, a 12° alcohol, 100 per cent varietal *mávro mesenikóla* wine made from free-run must of carefully selected grapes, fermented on skins only, and matured for two to three years in oak before bottling. About 3,000 hectolitres are made annually, but Erato is not released as vintage-dated wine. Its bright cherry-red colour is likely to please, and its light flavour can appeal as well. If Erato has a shortcoming, it must be that it is 'clean' to a fault, not quite suggesting that it has a place it calls home, much less one as individual as Agrafa. Plans call for deepening the colour and raising extract content by deriving 10–12 per cent of the must from either *petit syrah* or *cabernet sauvignon*, while also gaining an appellation of origin entitlement based on a like varietal formula. It remains to be seen, however, whether that step alone will contribute the facet Erato seems to lack. Perhaps a better result would be produced if the Union were also to realize their hope of eventually producing a reserve (*káva*) wine from *mávro mesenikóla* grapes grown only in the best vineyards of the semi-mountainous zone of Agrafa.

At this time, perhaps the more convincing proof of the quality inherent in the *mávro mesenikóla* is the Union's Rozé. Produced in an amount of nearly 2,000 hectolitres each year, it is an all-*mávro mesenikóla* rosé of free-run must. Firm and crisp, and with a characteristic fruit flavour, the orange-tinged Rozé is on a par with all but the very best rosé wines of Greece. Other wines of the Union, all of which appear under the Tavropos brand, include a pair each of red and white dry wines under the Lito and Nefeli labels, respectively the better and lesser. The reds are made in part with *mávro mesenikóla* must, but also *moskháto amvoúrgou*, as well as other red varieties grown to a small extent around Karditsa, such as *séfko (séfka/shevka)* and *senzó (cinsault)*. The whites are derived from *savatianó* and *batíki*. A retsina is produced exclusively from *savatianó*, and is among the few grown outside Central Greece that compares really well with the typical bottled retsinas of that region. The Union's wine offerings are completed by its Imiglyko, a semi-sweet red produced from *moskháto amvoúrgou*.

TYRNAVOS

The greatest concentration of Thessalian vineyards is in the north-easterly area around Tyrnavos, another country town, just to the north-west of the regional capital of Larisa. A Greek codex from 1792 indicates that the wines from this area had a good name, despite their origin on the plain. It should be noted as well, lest one think that Tyrnavos could have enjoyed its little bit of repute only among the miserable peasantry of Ottoman times, that the English traveller Leake wrote in 1835 that 'good wine' can be produced on the plain when attentive care is given. In Ottoman times, however, there was not much scope for exploiting the potential. The large Turkish agricultural estates, *chifliks*, typical of the plain, mostly produced grain. Even after the Greek state took control of Thessaly in 1881, economic conditions on the plain scarcely changed, Greek landlords merely replacing Turkish ones. Grapes could not compete with grain on their abacus either. The turning-point for viticulture, as for all other agricultural pursuits in Thessaly, was an agrarian uprising at the Kileler estate in 1910. Land distribution was begun in consequence, and only after that did conditions for wine-growing improve substantially.

The environment for viticulture is perhaps not quite so negative as one might think in taking a panoramic view of the Tyrnavos area. For one thing, elevation, at about 130 metres above sea level, is not quite so low as it might seem; also, upon closer examination, some incline is perceptible in places. The area is consequently not entirely at the mercy of blistering insolation or waterlogged soil. The soil, for that matter, is a sandy clay very suitable for the vine. The real Achilles' heel of the region seems to be, rather, its varietal complement. Of the nearly 3,000 hectares of vines now crowding Tyrnavos, the preponderant part is in the dual-purpose variety *moskháto amvoúrgou*, with a dwindling amount of *batíki* as well. The *savatianó* is the only significant wine grape. The Thessalian plain has grown mainly dessert grapes at least since Ottoman days, when the Turkish landlords had them cultivated for their table. Except for the introduction of the *savatianó* after phylloxera struck, there has been little tendency to break out of that pattern and seek suitable wine-grape varieties. On account of the use of *moskháto amvoúrgou* and *batíki* for wine, Tyrnavos is ineligible for an appellation of origin.

The bottled Tyrnavos wine deserving most attention is the dry red

61, produced by the Wine Cooperative of Tyrnavos, and named after the year in which the present winery was established. A limited-production wine, made in a quantity of about 500 hectolitres annually, 61 is the product exclusively of free-run juice of selected *moskháto amvoúrgou* grapes, a significant amount of which comes from the village of Damasi. It receives four to five years in oak before being bottled as a non-vintage wine. Alcohol is at 12.5°. A crimson rose-coloured wine of lightish body, 61 displays the marked softness typical of Tyrnavos wines, although it does linger finally to refresh with acidity. The aromatics are of an unabashedly perfumed flower-iness. Altogether, one may be reminded of that passage of *The Deipnosophists* in which it was said that the Thessalians 'emulated Persian luxury and extravagance' and were 'the most extravagant of all the Greeks in the matter both of clothing and food'. For some Westerners, 61 is not at all as red table wine ought to be.

The rosé and white companions in the Cooperative's trio of better wines are marketed respectively under the Maïstrali and Arletta labels, the first being another *moskháto amvoúrgou* wine, and the second a combination of *batíki* with the predominant *savatianó*. Lesser dry wines are whites labelled Areto and Lefkos, the rosé Kokkineli, and the red Erythros. The Cooperative also makes sweet red wines from the *moskháto amvoúrgou*, relying partially on concentrated must for sweetness, and grape spirits for alcohol. Fivos, of free-run must, and Ira, respectively the more and less fortified, are the fully sweet wines, while a lesser Imiglyko, a semi-sweet wine, is also produced. Enjoyment of them depends very greatly on their freshness in bottle, although even then their character as sweet muscat wines seems somewhat muted. A second producer of plains' wines, Vasdavanos Brothers, bottles dry white, rosé, and red wines under the Leda label, which seem to me to fall somewhere between the better and lesser wines of the respective types produced by the Cooperative. The Leda wines have not travelled securely beyond Piraeus.

PELION AND SKOPELOS

Another Thessalian area which, like Rapsani, had quite a reputation for its dry red wine in the past is Pelion, the mountainous peninsula and scenic gem of Magnisia, curving around to the south-east from

1 Samos (Eastern Sporades). Terraced vineyards of *moskháto áspro* in the north-central semi-mountainous zone.

2 Samos. A rainbow of muscat wine – from young dry wine from fresh grapes on the left, to aged sweet wine from partially raisined grapes on the right.

3 Rhodes (Dodecanese). Plantings of *athíri* on the flanks of Mt. Ataviros by Embouas.

4 Santorini (Cyclades). Vineyards on the island's inclined plateau, looking north from Fira.

5 Naousa (Macedonia). Rows of *xynómavro* at Yiannakokhori.

6 Rapsani (Thessaly). Vintage-time on the spines of Mt. Kissavos, the Ossa of the ancients.

7 Nemea (Peloponnesos). *Ayioryítiko* ripening in 'the deep valley of Nemea' (Pindar, *The Nemean Odes*)

8 Cephalonia (Ionian Islands). View southeast towards the island capital of Argostoli, from *robóla* vineyards in the appellation zone near Dilinata.